YORK NOTES

D0452896

LORD OF THE FLIES

WILLIAM GOLDING

NOTES BY S. W. FOSTER
REVISED BY BETH KEMP

PEARSON

YORK
PRESS

YORK PRESS
322 Old Brompton Road, London SW5 9JH

PEARSON EDUCATION LIMITED
Edinburgh Gate, Harlow,
Essex CM20 2JE, United Kingdom
Associated companies, branches and representatives throughout the world

First published 1997
New editions 2002 and 2010
This new and fully revised edition 2015

10 9 8 7 6 5 4 3 2 1

ISBN 978-1-4479-8219-7

Illustrated by Doreen Lang; and Moreno Chiacchiera (page 54 only)
Phototypeset by Carnegie Book Production
Printed in Slovakia

Photo credits: Michal Bednarek/Shutterstock for page 8 bottom / Jason Patrick Ross/Shutterstock for page 9 middle / deamles for sale/Shutterstock for page 19 bottom / Filip Fuxa/Shutterstock for page 23 bottom / 9comeback/Shutterstock for page 26 bottom / Peter Zijlstra/Shutterstock for page 28 bottom / Brian A Jackson/Shutterstock for page 31 bottom / Iakov Kalinin/Shutterstock for page 36 bottom / Dimedrol68/Shutterstock for page 38 bottom / Sabphoto/Shutterstock for page 40 bottom / goldenjack/ Shutterstock for page 41 bottom / ScandinavianStock/Shutterstock for page 46 middle / alarich/Shutterstock for page 48 bottom / Alex James Bramwell /Shutterstock for page 49 bottom / Ferenc Szelepcsenyi/Shutterstock for page 53 top / Angelo Giampiccolo/Shutterstock for page 56 bottom / PlusONE/Shutterstock for page 57 bottom / Jean-Regis Rouston/Roger Viollet/Getty for page 58 top / Lisa S./Shutterstock for page 58 bottom / yavuzunlu/Shutterstock for page 62 bottom / wavebreakmedia/Shutterstock for page 71 middle

CONTENTS

PART ONE:
GETTING STARTED

Preparing for assessment 5

How to use your York Notes Study Guide 6

PART TWO:
PLOT AND ACTION

Plot summary 8

Chapters One to Three 10

Chapters Four to Six 16

Chapters Seven to Ten 22

Chapters Eleven to Twelve 30

Progress and revision check 35

PART THREE:
CHARACTERS

Who's who? 37

Ralph 38

Jack 40

Piggy 42

Simon 43

Roger and Maurice 44

Sam and Eric 45

Minor characters 46

Progress and revision check 47

PART FOUR:
THEMES, CONTEXTS AND SETTINGS

Themes...48

Contexts..52

Settings...53

Progress and revision check............................55

PART FIVE:
FORM, STRUCTURE AND LANGUAGE

Form..56

Structure...57

Language...58

Progress and revision check............................61

PART SIX:
PROGRESS BOOSTER

Understanding the question 62

Planning your answer 62

Responding to writers' effects 64

Using quotations...66

Spelling, punctuation and grammar................67

Annotated sample answers..............................68

Practice task and further questions 74

PART SEVEN:
FURTHER STUDY AND ANSWERS

Literary terms 75

Checkpoint answers..76

Progress and revision check answers 77

Mark scheme 80

PART ONE: GETTING STARTED

PREPARING FOR ASSESSMENT

HOW WILL I BE ASSESSED ON MY WORK ON *LORD OF THE FLIES?*

All exam boards are different but whichever course you are following, your work will be examined through these four Assessment Objectives:

Assessment Objectives	Wording	Worth thinking about ...
A01	Read, understand and respond to texts. Students should be able to: • maintain a critical style and develop an informed personal response • use textual references, including quotations, to support and illustrate interpretations.	• How well do I know what happens, what people say, do etc.? • What do *I* think about the key ideas in the play? • How can I support my viewpoint in a really convincing way? • What are the best quotations to use and when should I use them?
A02	Analyse the language, form and structure used by a writer to create meanings and effects, using relevant subject terminology where appropriate.	• What specific things does the writer 'do'? What choices has Golding made? (Why this particular word, phrase or paragraph here? Why does this event happen at this point?) • What effects do these choices create? (Suspense? Ironic laughter? Reflective mood?)
A03	Show understanding of the relationships between texts and the contexts in which they were written.	• What can I learn about society from the book? (What does it tell me about class divisions in Golding's day, for example?) • What was society like in Golding's time? Can I see it reflected in the story?
A04	Use a range of vocabulary and sentence structures for clarity, purpose and effect, with accurate spelling and punctuation.	• How accurately and clearly do I write? • Are there small errors of grammar, spelling and punctuation I can get rid of?

Look out for the Assessment Objective labels throughout your York Notes Study Guide – these will help to focus your study and revision!

The text used in this Study Guide is the Faber and Faber paperback edition, 1958.

HOW TO USE YOUR YORK NOTES STUDY GUIDE

You are probably wondering what is the best and most efficient way to use your York Notes Study Guide on *Lord of the Flies*. Here are three possibilities:

A **step-by-step** study and revision guide	A **'dip-in' support** when you need it	A **revision guide** after you have finished the novel
Step 1: Read Part Two as you read the novel, as a companion to help you study it. **Step 2:** When you need to, turn to Parts Three to Five to focus your learning. **Step 3:** Then, when you have finished, use Parts Six and Seven to hone your exam skills, revise and practise for the exam.	Perhaps you know the book quite well, but you want to check your understanding and practise your exam skills? Just look for the section you think you need most help with and go for it!	You might want to use the Notes after you have finished your study, using Parts Two to Five to check over what you have learned, and then work through Parts Six and Seven in the immediate weeks leading up to your exam.

HOW WILL THE GUIDE HELP YOU STUDY AND REVISE?

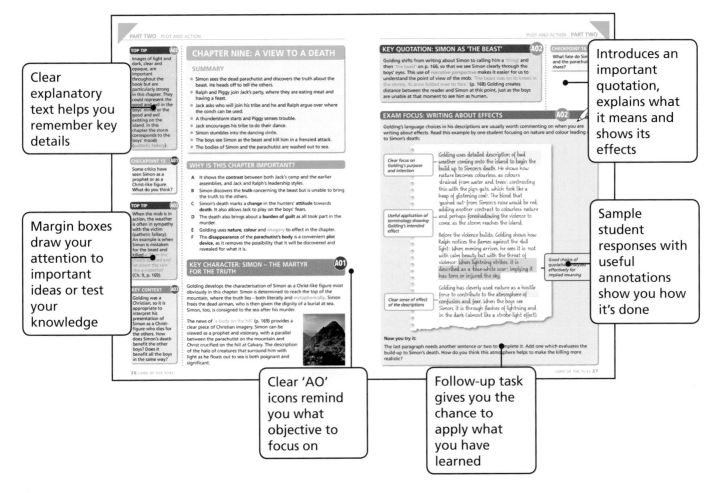

Clear explanatory text helps you remember key details

Margin boxes draw your attention to important ideas or test your knowledge

Introduces an important quotation, explains what it means and shows its effects

Sample student responses with useful annotations show you how it's done

Clear 'AO' icons remind you what objective to focus on

Follow-up task gives you the chance to apply what you have learned

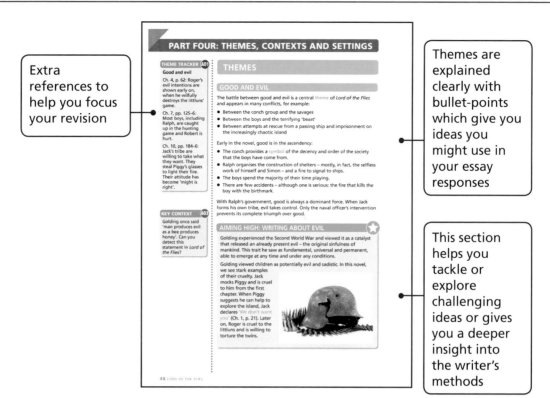

Extra references to help you focus your revision

Themes are explained clearly with bullet-points which give you ideas you might use in your essay responses

This section helps you tackle or explore challenging ideas or gives you a deeper insight into the writer's methods

Parts Two to Five each end with a **Progress and Revision Check**:

A set of quick questions tests your knowledge of the text

Further substantial and 'open' tasks test your understanding

Self-evaluation – so you can keep a record of how you are getting on

Don't forget Parts Six and Seven, with advice and practice on **improving your writing skills**:

- Focus on **difficult areas** such as **'context'** and **'inferences'**
- **Short snippets** of **other students' work** to show you how it's done (or not done!)
- Three annotated **sample responses** to a task **at different levels**, with **expert comments**, to help you judge your own level
- **Practice questions**
- **Answers** to the **Progress and Revision Checks** and **Checkpoint** margin boxes

Now it's up to you! Don't forget – there's even more help on our website with more sample answers, essay planners and even online tutorials. Go to www.yorknotes.com to find out more.

PLOT SUMMARY: WHAT HAPPENS IN *LORD OF THE FLIES?*

REVISION FOCUS: GETTING THE PLOT STRAIGHT

Create a timeline showing the main events of the plot in order. Do not worry about exact timings, as these are not always clear in the novel. The important thing is to get the most important events into your timeline in the correct order. You could extend this by annotating it to show the development of themes and characters, perhaps using a colour code to help you organise the ideas and produce a useful revision tool.

CHAPTERS ONE AND TWO: ESTABLISHING ORDER ON THE ISLAND

TOP TIP (A01)

Although knowing the plot may seem less important than more demanding literary analysis, understanding what happens and in what order can help you to think about how themes and characters are developed.

- A group of boys are evacuated because of a war involving England. They become marooned on a small island.
- Ralph and Piggy meet and find a conch. Ralph blows the conch to call other survivors, who gather together on the beach.
- A group of choirboys arrive, led by Jack Merridew. They are mostly older boys.
- Ralph is elected leader but Jack is not pleased. Jack and his choir become the hunters.
- Ralph, Jack and Simon explore the island. Jack almost kills a piglet.
- A meeting is called. The conch becomes a symbol of authority.
- The boys argue over the existence of a beast on the island.
- A fire is lit to attract attention but it burns out of control. A boy with a birthmark disappears.

CHAPTERS THREE AND FOUR: ORDER IS SLIPPING

- Jack takes delight in tracking pigs but fails to kill any.
- Ralph constructs shelters but with only limited success due to lack of help.
- Jack and Ralph argue over priorities.
- Simon goes into the forest alone.
- Roger and Maurice destroy the smaller children's sandcastles. Roger throws stones at Henry.
- Ralph spots a ship. The chance of rescue disappears because the fire is left unattended.
- The hunters return with a pig. Ralph is angry with Jack for letting the fire go out.
- Feeling guilty, Jack lashes out at Piggy and smashes a lens in his glasses.
- Ralph is upset and calls a meeting.

CHAPTERS FIVE AND SIX: FOCUSING ON THE BEAST

- Ralph points out the requirements for survival.
- Discussion turns to the 'beastie', which Jack and Piggy dismiss.
- Unseen by the boys, a dead parachutist drifts onto the island near the fire.
- Sam and Eric believe he is the beast and rush to tell the others.
- The boys gather on the platform and Jack suggests they hunt the beast.
- Ralph, Jack and the older boys head off together. Piggy stays behind with the 'littluns'.
- Ralph goes alone to the unexplored part of a rocky outcrop where he is soon joined by Jack.

CHAPTERS SEVEN AND EIGHT: THRILL OF THE HUNT

- Ralph notices how dirty the boys have become.
- Ralph and the hunters try to kill a wild boar and re-enact the event.
- Ralph, Jack and Roger hunt for the beast on the mountain-top. They see the dead parachutist, and think he is the beast.
- The boys discuss the beast. Jack believes the hunters can kill it. Ralph knows they are just boys armed with sticks.
- Jack unsuccessfully tries to overthrow Ralph as leader. He wanders off, soon secretly joined by many of the older boys.
- The hunters kill a sow. They plan to invite the others to a feast with the aim of stealing their fire, and they put the pig's head on a stick.
- Simon has a 'conversation' with the pig's head, then falls unconscious.

CHAPTERS NINE AND TEN: SAVAGERY RULES

- Simon sees the dead parachutist and knows the truth about the beast.
- Ralph and Piggy join the other boys' feast. They dance and chant as thunder strikes.
- Simon stumbles into the tribal circle. He is seen as the beast and killed in a frenzied attack.
- Simon and the parachutist are washed out to sea.
- Ralph, Piggy, Sam and Eric show signs of guilt. Ralph becomes confused.
- Jack and his hunters set up camp on the rocky outcrop.
- Three hunters attack Piggy at night and steal his glasses.

CHAPTERS ELEVEN AND TWELVE: CHAOS AND RESCUE

- Ralph, Piggy, Sam and Eric decide to confront Jack.
- Piggy is killed by a falling rock when Roger leans on a lever, catapulting the rock towards him. The conch is also destroyed.
- Sam and Eric are captured by the hunters, leaving Ralph alone.
- Jack and his hunters track Ralph as if he is a pig.
- Jack sets most of the island on fire in order to flush out Ralph.
- As Ralph collapses on the beach, he sees a naval officer. He is rescued!

TOP TIP **A01**

An effective way to make your plot outline more detailed and useful is to annotate events with the symbols or allegorical ideas they relate to. This will help you to see how ideas are developed throughout the novel.

CHAPTER ONE: THE SOUND OF THE SHELL

SUMMARY

- A group of boys are marooned on an island after evacuation from a war zone.
- Ralph and Piggy are first on the scene and use a conch to summon other survivors.
- The most impressive entrance is made by a group of choirboys led by the red-haired Jack Merridew, head boy and chapter chorister.
- One of the choirboys, Simon, faints near the platform where the boys are gathering.
- Piggy's nickname is revealed to the boys' general amusement.
- The boys elect Ralph as chief. Jack believes the role should be his. He and Ralph agree that the choir will be the hunters, with Jack in charge.
- Ralph, Jack and Simon decide to explore the island.
- The three boys come across a piglet, which Jack almost kills before hesitating. He declares he will spill blood 'Next time—!' (p. 29).

WHY IS THIS CHAPTER IMPORTANT?

A It establishes the **setting** – a desert island.

B Golding introduces us to the main characters – Ralph, Piggy, Jack, Simon and Roger – and aspects of their different personalities are revealed.

C After Ralph is elected **leader**, we learn of his generosity when he asks Jack to take charge of the hunters.

D The importance of the **conch** is established and it becomes a symbol of authority.

E The **bad weather** on the island foreshadows later events, when Simon is murdered.

TOP TIP (A03)

Think about what is happening in the adult world. Adults are destroying each other in an all-out war, using every weapon available to them. This foreshadows later events: the boys will destroy much of the island.

TOP TIP (A01)

Read your exam question with care. If it is about the setting and the island, stick to these elements. Also make sure you understand vocabulary in the text: it may be useful to make yourself a glossary of unfamiliar words that Golding uses.

KEY SETTING: THE ISLAND   (A02)

In this chapter Golding clearly establishes the island setting as a tropical paradise with danger underlying its beauty. Notice the vivid, physical terms he uses to portray its richness and variety – 'defiles', 'cirque', 'reef', 'lagoon', 'scar' (pp. 24–7). The threatening aspect of the island is seen immediately when 'a bird, a vision of red and yellow, flashed upwards with a witch-like cry' (p. 1). You will see that the island is one of many contrasts – high and low, rocky and forested, friendly and unfriendly. It is also 'roughly boat-shaped' (p. 26) – tapering towards one end.

KEY CHARACTERS: RALPH, PIGGY AND JACK   (A01)

Golding introduces the main characters straight away, and begins to show us their differences. Ralph and Piggy are the first boys we encounter. Ralph is clearly more relaxed on the island, taking the opportunity to go for a swim in the tropical heat. Golding develops Piggy's character by showing how he tries to be friendly, confiding to Ralph that 'Piggy' is a nickname.

Piggy is fat, suffers from asthma and is far from physically fit. However, he thinks and acts like an adult and makes intelligent suggestions to Ralph, such as 'We ought to have a meeting' (p. 5). Ralph is able to put Piggy's ideas into action.

Jack is head chorister and sees himself as a natural leader. When Piggy proposes that they make a list of names, Jack ridicules his list. This foreshadows later events, when Jack shows his intense dislike for Piggy.

KEY QUOTATION: JACK'S CHARACTER   (A01)

Jack's impatience with words and ideas is shown when he snaps at Piggy: '"You're talking too much," said Jack Merridew, "Shut up, Fatty."' (p. 17) This reveals his preference for action over thought, and highlights a key contrast between him and Piggy.

AIMING HIGH: WRITING ABOUT THE BOYS' NAMES   ⭐

Many aspects of this novel are symbolic or allegorical, and one way to demonstrate a subtle understanding is to approach the text at this level. The ways Golding uses naming is worth discussion in this respect. For example, the novel begins 'The boy with fair hair' (p. 1), and we later learn that this is Ralph. Introducing the character without a name helps the reader to see him less as an individual to start with. Jack's surname is revealed as Merridew but we are not told many boys' surnames. Piggy is so named because of his appearance. Have you noticed that we never learn his true name?

The lack of names, and lack of individuality this creates, supports Golding's intention to create an allegorical novel. Having characters who are more types than individuals makes it easier for the reader to interpret the text's universal message rather than seeing it as a story about specific, particular boys.

TOP TIP   (A01)

Look at the detail. For example, Jack does not kill the pig because he is not yet far enough removed from civilisation. Later, he will do so! Another detail is the way in which Piggy is influenced by adults – mostly his aunt.

CHECKPOINT 1   (A01)

How many of the boys' surnames do we know?

CHAPTER TWO: FIRE ON THE MOUNTAIN

SUMMARY

- The three explorers – Ralph, Jack and Simon – return and Ralph blows the conch to call a meeting. He confirms they are on an uninhabited island.
- Jack points out that an army is required for hunting, while Ralph is more concerned with immediate practical issues.
- Ralph and Jack agree that rules are needed. Ralph is concerned about order, while Jack is excited at the idea of punishing rule-breakers.
- The younger boys (the 'littluns') express their concern about a 'beastie' (p. 35) on the island.
- At Ralph's suggestion, the boys agree to start a fire to attract the attention of passing ships.
- A fire lit on the mountain-top using Piggy's glasses burns out of control.
- Jack offers to keep the fire going – ordering his hunters to work in rotation.
- Piggy tells the boys they need to 'act proper' (p. 45) if they are to be rescued.
- Piggy discovers the boy with the birthmark has disappeared.

CHECKPOINT 2 **A01**

What is the 'beastie' called at first?

WHY IS THIS CHAPTER IMPORTANT?

A   It establishes the idea that a **beast** might lurk on the island.

B   Ralph and Jack's different **priorities** are shown.

C   Golding introduces the idea of lighting a **fire** as a main way of being rescued. This will be important throughout the story.

D   The agreement that the **hunters** watch over the fire will break down later in the novel.

E   The first **death** occurs, through the boys' carelessness. This death foreshadows later tragedies.

TOP TIP **A01**

Ralph and Jack get on well in this chapter. They grin at each other and share 'that strange invisible light of friendship' (p. 39). Look out for any evidence in the coming chapters that shows the deterioration of their relationship.

KEY QUOTATION: RALPH'S CHARACTER **A02**

Golding develops Ralph's character in this chapter as a practical boy, who takes a straightforward and commonsense approach to problems and assumes that others will agree with him. This is shown through the simplicity of his language when he informs the others that 'There aren't any grown-ups. We shall have to look after ourselves.' (p. 31) This demonstrates his focus on practicalities, while the lack of connectives or supporting argument shows that he sees no need to try to persuade the others of his view.

KEY THEME: FIRE

Golding introduces the need for a fire in this chapter. The fire has two purposes – it is a practical aid to the boys' rescue and a source of fun. Under normal circumstances boys between six and twelve years of age would not be entrusted with fire, even with adult supervision, and certainly not on this scale. Notice how the atmosphere changes when the fire becomes not fun but fatal.

KEY CHARACTER: PIGGY (A02)

Piggy's role as the most adult-like boy, and representative of reason, is clearly developed in this chapter. While most of the boys see the potential for enjoyment of the fire, Piggy sees its possible dangers. His manner and tone in this chapter are almost parental: 'My! You've made a big heap, haven't you?' (p. 40). He also urges the need for practical considerations, like shelters, after the cold of the previous night.

> **TOP TIP** (A02)
>
> Look at the language Golding uses to describe Jack's treatment of Piggy. What does his choice of words tell you?

EXAM FOCUS: WRITING ABOUT THE BEAST (A03)

You may be asked to write about symbolic aspects of the novel. Read this example by one student, focused on the significance of the beast.

> *Clear focus on the beast's significance in the novel as a whole*

> *Clear link to a further, more detailed point*

Golding uses the beast to represent evil and to show that, ultimately, evil is within us all. In this part of the novel, where the beast is introduced, it serves to emphasise divisions between the boys. The older boys dismiss the idea of a 'beastie' as a figment of the younger boys' imaginations, and one of the older boys points out that the little boy with the birthmark 'must have had a nightmare'. As well as showing these divisions between groups of boys, Golding uses the idea of the beast to further develop the differences between Ralph and Jack. Ralph is frustrated that the boys will not accept that 'You couldn't have a beastie ... on an island this size.', while Jack assures 'the littleuns' that his hunters would kill it if it did exist.

> *Use of connective emphasises the contrast between the two boys*

Now you try it:

This paragraph needs a sentence or two to link it all together, by referring back to the initial idea of the beast representing evil within us all. You could use the information on Golding's personal experiences in **Part Four: Contexts** to help you.

CHAPTER THREE: HUTS ON THE BEACH

SUMMARY

- Jack goes pig hunting – unsuccessfully.
- Ralph shows his sense of responsibility by attempting to build shelters, but these are only partially successful because of lack of help from the rest of the boys, apart from Simon.
- Jack develops a fascination for hunting pigs.
- Ralph and Jack have a difference of opinion; Jack's obsession with hunting irritates Ralph, who is more concerned with the general well-being of the boys.
- Ralph views Jack's hunting as enjoyment.
- Simon goes off into the forest on his own.

WHY IS THIS CHAPTER IMPORTANT?

CHECKPOINT 3 **A01**

What evidence is there that Jack is fully focused on hunting?

A Golding further develops **Ralph's** character. We see how concerned Ralph is with **practical** matters – mainly keeping a fire burning and constructing shelters.

B We learn more about **Simon**.

C With virtually all the boys doing what they want, this foreshadows later events, when the boys willingly turn to **savagery**.

D We witness Jack's growing **fascination** with hunting pigs – that he is willing to spill blood and he enjoys the **thrill of the hunt**.

E We see how some boys act on the **vows** made at the assembly, while others are content to **survive** day by day.

KEY THEME: LAW AND ORDER **A01**

Golding emphasises the importance of order and organisation in this chapter. The boys have come from a society in which orderliness is normal and attempt to continue this when they first arrive on the island.

Very quickly, the conch has come to symbolise the values of their previous existence. The boys cannot talk at meetings unless they are holding the conch. They must treat whoever is speaking with respect.

This means that Piggy, despite being in many ways a natural victim, is able to air intelligent thoughts that lead to improvements in the boys' lives, for example moving the toilets away from the shelters and keeping a fire going.

'Parliaments' of this kind have always been key elements of successful civilisations. It is Jack who challenges this structure. His leadership is more like that of a dictator.

KEY QUOTATION: SIMON'S CHARACTER **A02**

The complexity of Simon's character is developed here. For example, Golding tells us that 'his eyes [were] so bright they had deceived Ralph into thinking him delightfully gay and wicked.' (p. 57) The idea that his appearance had tricked Ralph shows that Simon is not easy to work out, and that Ralph does not entirely understand him.

Although Simon helps with the shelters, he also likes to be alone. At the end of this chapter, Ralph and Jack expect to find Simon in the pool with the others. However, he has gone into the forest with 'an air of purpose' (p. 57).

AIMING HIGH: WRITING ABOUT PIGGY'S GLASSES

It is important that you can discuss how Golding uses Piggy's glasses as a symbol in different ways throughout the novel as a whole.

First, they expose the breakdown of law and order. They belong to Piggy, who needs them to see properly. Used with permission, they start the fires that are seen as essential both for rescue and for hygienically cooked food.

In later chapters, Jack refuses to respect Piggy's right to the glasses – first punching him and breaking a lens, then stealing them to light fires. Jack is challenging Ralph's style of leadership, which has kept things reasonable on the island.

Second, Piggy's glasses also represent the idea of possession or ownership – what belongs to whom. By using Piggy's glasses to start the fire, Jack replaces the rule of law with personal desire and need.

Finally, they also contribute to the irony in the novel, as Piggy is unable to see clearly without them, yet is able to 'see' the truth better than any of the others.

KEY CONTEXT **A03**

Golding's novel is partly a reaction to a Victorian book called *The Coral Island* (R. M. Ballantyne, 1857) in which marooned British children bring civilised order into a wilderness. Golding thought the story was unrealistic and that groups of children do not behave as the book depicted.

TOP TIP **A02**

Evaluate the part played by the hunters in the story so far. Who do they see as leader? Notice how their allegiance to Jack develops as the story progresses.

CHECKPOINT 4 **A01**

What are the hunters doing while Jack is still looking for pigs?

CHAPTER FOUR: PAINTED FACES AND LONG HAIR

SUMMARY

- The littluns play on the beach but their play is disturbed by Roger and Maurice, who destroy their sandcastles. Roger throws stones close to Henry.
- Jack paints his face with clay and charcoal and goes hunting.
- Ralph spies the smoke of a ship on the horizon.
- He discovers the fire has gone out.
- The hunters return with a dead pig.
- Ralph is angry and Piggy backs him up. Jack smashes a lens in Piggy's glasses.
- Ralph, upset about the fire going out, calls a meeting.

WHY IS THIS CHAPTER IMPORTANT?

A Roger's **cruelty** comes to light.

B With the **successful hunt** – the first occasion where blood is spilt – we are allowed a glimpse into possible **further events**, when human blood is spilt.

C The chance of a **rescue** is **lost** and so the boys are given time to descend into **savagery**.

D In the hunters' chant and re-enactment of the kill we see a **de-civilising process** emerging.

E Attitudes towards **Piggy** are further exposed, and Golding shows the growing **division** between Jack and Ralph.

TOP TIP (A01)

Golding shows Roger to be a cruel character during the course of the novel. Here, his cruelty is portrayed for the first time as he destroys the three littluns' sandcastles and kicks sand into Percival's eye. What motive does he have, if any?

CHECKPOINT 5 (A01)

Who mimics Roger's cruelty?

KEY CHARACTERS: PIGGY (A02)

Golding clearly presents others' attitudes towards Piggy at various points in this chapter, showing aspects of their characters at the same time.

Generally speaking, the others see Piggy as 'an outsider' (p. 68). His accent is different, less middle-class than the other boys'. His size, his asthma and the fact that he wears glasses set him apart. He is of little help in hunting or building shelters, which reinforces the view that he is different and useless.

Ralph's practicality can be seen in his attitude to Piggy. At first, Ralph considers Piggy in a negative light, believing him to be 'a bore' (p. 68). At this point in the novel, Ralph thinks Piggy's ideas are 'dull' (p. 68) and he smiles at the prospect of 'pulling his leg'. However, he will soon recognise Piggy's value to the group, and to himself as leader.

Jack's violent and aggressive nature is highlighted when he uses Piggy as an easy target to express his frustrations in this chapter. When Jack breaks his promise by letting the fire go out, he is unable to face up to his failure. He realises that the possibility of rescue is far more important than hunting. He is confronted by Ralph and also criticised by Piggy, and he lashes out at the easier target – Piggy – breaking a lens in his glasses.

When the boys cook and eat the pig, Piggy asks for meat but Jack points out that he is not entitled to any because he did not hunt. Simon, feeling guilty about not having hunted either, gives his meat to Piggy, showing Simon's inherent goodness and sense of fairness.

KEY THEME: ORDER AND CHAOS (A01)

In this chapter, Golding shows the growing gap between Ralph and Jack, representing the gulf between order and chaos. Ralph's link to order and civilisation is strengthened through his despair at the passing of the ship, as well as his focus on working towards the longer-term goal of survival until rescue. Ralph is beginning to lose the idea of being on the island as fun.

Jack, on the other hand, allows his desire to hunt to absorb him and, even when he recognises that he has acted rashly, he is proud and aggressive in the incident involving Piggy. He apologises for letting the fire go out but not, significantly, for breaking the glasses. Jack's use of face paint shows how he is becoming less civilised: 'the mask was a thing on its own, behind which Jack hid, liberated from shame and self-consciousness' (p. 66).

REVISION FOCUS: TRACKING THE DESCENT INTO CHAOS

It is very important that you can explain how certain events show the gradual descent into chaos in the novel, so that you can write about this effectively in the exam. Create a diagram (for example, a flow chart or a timeline) to record what these key moments are and how they show the boys moving away from civilisation. Once you have produced this diagram, you can use it to test yourself on this theme.

TOP TIP (A01)

Do you think that the choice of Piggy's name is significant? If you have the chance in the exam, get these small points across – it will show you know the book well.

TOP TIP (A02)

Notice how many of the boys are now caught up in the hunt and are losing their ties to civilisation and order. Golding demonstrates this in the simplicity of the language they use in the rhythmic and repetitive three-syllable chant: 'Kill the pig. Cut her throat. Bash her in.' (p. 79).

CHECKPOINT 6 (A01)

Why is Jack so keen to have meat on an island rich in fruit and shellfish?

CHAPTER FIVE: BEAST FROM WATER

SUMMARY

- Ralph thinks about the seriousness of the forthcoming meeting and of his role as chief.
- At the meeting, he lays down the ground rules for behaviour on the island.
- Discussion turns to the beast, and some of the boys wonder if they are not alone on the island. Jack and Piggy dismiss the idea.
- The opinions of Piggy and Simon are ignored.
- Jack and Ralph have a further disagreement and the meeting ends.
- Simon and Piggy, fearing what Jack is capable of, urge Ralph to remain as chief.
- Simon, Piggy and Ralph discuss what grown-ups would do, and wish for a signal from them.

WHY IS THIS CHAPTER IMPORTANT?

A   Golding's **description** on the first page of this chapter **mirrors** Ralph's **feelings**, and we see his increasing unease.

B   As Ralph begins to recognise the qualities needed for **leadership**, we notice his new **respect** for Piggy.

C   It is significant that Jack **dismisses** the idea of a **beast** here, for he will later use the boys' fear of it to his own **advantage**.

D   Piggy's **logical thinking** and knowledge of **science** lead him to argue that the only **fear** worth considering is the fear of **people** – an important idea in the novel.

E   Simon would like to speak about the **nature of evil** but he is silenced – which foreshadows his death later on, when he tries to bring the truth about the beast to the boys.

KEY CHARACTER: RALPH AS LEADER

In this chapter, Golding shows how Ralph is forced to grow up quickly as life takes on a new seriousness for him. He walks on the beach thinking about the boys' initial enthusiasm for the island. He considers how their original ideas for keeping order have broken down and realises that prospects for rescue in the immediate future are not good.

Having decided to call an assembly, he is anxious that it does not turn into a pointless exercise and a wasted opportunity. He thinks beforehand, 'This meeting must not be fun, but business' (p. 81).

CHECKPOINT 7 A01

What particularly worries Ralph about the boys' adjustment to life on the island?

TOP TIP A01

Ralph points out that 'the rules are the only thing we've got!' (p. 99). How far have the rules of civilised society broken down at this stage? It is a useful exercise to track the breakdown of the rules as you go through each chapter.

Before speaking at the assembly, Ralph considers the weight of his responsibility as chief. He recognises being able to think rationally and systematically as an important requirement for leadership, showing his connection to the theme of order or civilisation. He realises that Piggy is able to think clearly and logically and begins to have a new-found respect for him.

KEY THEME: EVIL (A02)

Golding uses this chapter to show how the boys' fears take shape as the beast: they focus on possible external sources of evil. Although the chapter is called 'Beast from Water', in 'deciding on the fear' (p. 88) a number of explanations are put forward.

The explanations range from real wild creatures, like the giant squid, to humans themselves being the source of fear. Unreal phenomena are also considered – fear created by the imagination, fear of evil and fear of ghosts. Notice how each suggestion is received by the different boys.

The significance of the chapter is that it creates doubt in the minds of the boys that they are alone and introduces the possibility of something 'other' on the island: an evil presence which is separate from them.

CHECKPOINT 8 (A01)

Why might Piggy be fearful of people?

AIMING HIGH: WRITING ABOUT VIEWS ON RALPH AS LEADER ★

For a high mark, you may need to view one of the boys through the eyes of other characters. Knowing a variety of viewpoints on a particular person is important as together they will give a balanced insight into the author's presentation of a character's personality.

Jack lacks respect both for the authority of the conch and for Ralph as leader. This leads Jack to break the rules. When confronted by Ralph, he shouts and swears. Golding uses bad language to demonstrate his contempt for any sort of authority.

Piggy, on the other hand, sees Ralph as a good and natural leader, but fears for his own position if Ralph lost power. He is afraid of what Jack might do if Jack became leader.

Simon is clear and straightforward in his statement that Ralph should remain as leader: 'Go on being chief' (p. 101).

TOP TIP (A01)

To aim for a top grade, you will need to know how the characters shape and react to events. For example, notice how Jack and Piggy treat the younger boys when the fear of the beast is mentioned. Who is kinder?

CHAPTER SIX: BEAST FROM AIR

SUMMARY

- A dead parachutist drifts onto the island.
- As Sam and Eric tend the fire, they mistake the parachutist for the beast.
- At a meeting, Jack announces that the beast should be hunted down and he ridicules the importance of the conch.
- The bigger boys, without Piggy, set off to find the beast.
- Ralph bravely goes first to the unexplored part of a rocky outcrop. He is soon joined by Jack.
- The boys discover that the end of the island would be a good place for a fort.
- Ralph stresses the boys' practical needs and the others reluctantly go on with their journey.

CHECKPOINT 9 **A01**

What is the significance of the parachutist?

WHY IS THIS CHAPTER IMPORTANT?

A   The **dead parachutist** is seen as the **beast**, which has huge implications for the group.

B   The role of **Sam** and **Eric**, speaking as **one voice**, is evident in this chapter. Their description of the beast is terrifying – more so because of the two boys' simultaneous account.

C   The revelation that the **beast** exists is reassuring as it is now **recognised** as real, something that can be hunted. This reinforces the **importance** of Jack's hunters.

D   The **conch** loses importance as the need to hunt down the beast now dominates the boys' minds. Golding shows us **Ralph's leadership qualities** and **bravery** in action.

E   The **differences** between Jack and Piggy are further highlighted.

F   Simon begins to **understand** the **true nature** of the beast.

TOP TIP **A02**

When commenting on Golding's use of description, point out that his natural descriptions are mingled with events. The first two paragraphs of this chapter set the scene and action. Golding writes 'A sliver of moon rose over the horizon' (p. 103), going on to describe the battle from the vantage point of the island. Notice 'but there were other lights in the sky, that moved fast, winked, or went out' (p. 103).

KEY THEME: THE BEAST

Here Golding reminds readers of the world beyond the island, and invokes some of the fears of the 1950s.

The boys wanted a sign from the grown-ups but do not get what they expected. Above them a battle is being fought and a 'sign' comes down in the form of a parachutist. In the novel, the world of grown-ups is a fearful place, involved in a war using the atomic bomb, greatly feared when Golding was writing. This chapter reminds us that the grown-ups are doing no better than their sons. Sending a 'beast' as a sign is, therefore, appropriate.

Ralph's willingness to call an assembly as soon as the twins tell him their news shows that he is aware of the near panic of the previous evening. The twins' description of what they saw terrifies the other boys. Jack, though, suddenly has new power. There is no longer a debate about whether the hunters are needed: they are now defenders!

KEY CHARACTERS: DIFFERENT REACTIONS TO THE BEAST

Golding uses the beast to reveal the boys' key characteristics. Jack is delighted at the prospect of a hunt. At last, the power is shifting his way. He is able to ridicule Piggy's fear of the beast and the importance of the conch, seeing the ritual of holding the conch to speak to the assembly as pointless and unproductive.

It is Jack who initially leads Ralph and the bigger boys in search of the beast. They look around the tail end of the island – the only part Jack previously failed to visit. Jack is aggressive, physically able and impulsive.

Piggy is not physically active. However, he is intelligent and able to express his ideas and opinions. Despite dismissing ghosts earlier, he admits to being frightened, suggesting that they stay where they are rather than search for the beast.

TOP TIP: WRITING ABOUT POWER AND LEADERSHIP

An example of Ralph's developing leadership can be seen in this chapter. After the meeting, Piggy urges Ralph to 'blow the conch' (p. 99) to restore order and call the boys back, but Ralph recognises that risking the conch being ignored is dangerous: 'If I blow the conch and they don't come back ... we've had it.' (p. 99). Ralph understands that chaos is breaking through and knows that getting rid of it altogether would be impossible, so it is safer to let it run its course and try again another time.

Although Piggy is the representative of logic and clear thinking, here it is fear which governs his thoughts. This shows that Ralph understands people better than Piggy. This trait is part of his practicality which makes him a more suitable leader.

TOP TIP A01

Simon emerges as a complex and important minor character. Despite the fact that he says and does comparatively little, his speech and actions are highly significant. Take careful note of what happens whenever his name is mentioned.

KEY CONTEXT A03

Golding was interested in books on psychology. This allowed him to create convincing characters, even while using them as symbols or types in allegory. We can see that his characters have depth, because they each have a strong emotion that motivates them, for example Piggy is motivated by fear, Jack by pride. What motivates Ralph?

CHAPTER SEVEN: SHADOWS AND TALL TREES

SUMMARY

- Ralph is dismayed by the dirty state of the boys and considers the harsher terrain of the other side of the island.
- Simon tries to reassure Ralph that he'll get home safely.
- Jack discovers the tracks of a wild boar.
- The boys make up a ritual dance to celebrate the hunt. They claim it is just a game, but Robert is hurt.
- Ralph, Jack and Roger hunt for the beast on the mountain-top. They discover the dead parachutist, whom they assume is the beast.
- Terrified by their discovery, they flee down the mountain.

WHY IS THIS CHAPTER IMPORTANT?

A We see further evidence of the boys' **decline** through **Ralph's observations** about their lack of cleanliness.

B We witness Ralph's awe at the immensity and power of the **ocean**, which he sees as a **barrier** between the island and the civilised world.

C Ralph's **reflections** on the **comforts** of his typically English middle-class home provide a contrast between the **civilised adult world** and the **island**. There is a sense of **loss**.

D The boys' playful **re-enactment** of their hunt is yet further evidence of their descent into **savagery**.

E Golding develops the theme of **leadership**, as Jack and Ralph try to prove their **courage** and right to lead.

KEY LANGUAGE: NATURAL IMAGES (A02)

Golding makes plentiful use of natural images and descriptions in this chapter. For example, Ralph's continuing thoughts about the vastness of the sea (see Chapter 6) are repeated at greater length. The description of the forest is vivid, the undergrowth on one side is impassable, the sea and the cliffs on the other are threatening, showing the reader 'the divider, the barrier' (p. 121) between the world of adults and the boys' world. Golding uses a three-part list to show how Ralph cannot help but recognise the fact that the boys are trapped on the island: 'one was clamped down, one was helpless, one was condemned.' (p. 121)

Ralph earlier called the island 'good' (Ch. 2, p. 33) but in this chapter the natural forces appear hostile. Ralph is able to understand the power of the sea against humanity. The sea has the power to 'suck down' (p. 120). As the boys' situation becomes more threatening, so do their surroundings. While initially there was a balance of comforting and frightening descriptions of the island, that balance is now shifting.

KEY THEME: SAVAGERY AND TRIBALISM

The acting out of the hunt is reminiscent of tribal dances which are a ritualistic representation of a successful hunt that the tribe hopes for in the future. This, coupled with Jack's mask and the rallying chant of earlier chapters, highlights the move away from conventional behaviour or civilisation and towards savagery. It also shows us the descent into paganism, i.e. beliefs outside the main world religions.

At first, the enactment is controlled, the boys were 'all jabbing at Robert who made mock rushes' (p. 125). Soon, 'Robert was screaming and struggling with the strength of frenzy' (p. 125), and is eventually reduced to 'frightened snivels' (p. 125).

Notice how the enactment almost gets out of control. Even Ralph is 'carried away' (p. 125) by the moment. Golding suggests that the desire to hunt and kill is deep within the male human psyche, making Simon's murder believable in a later chapter.

The sentences in this part of the chapter are short and interspersed with short speeches, which are either pleas or commands: language is breaking down along with civilisation.

TOP TIP: WRITING ABOUT THE USE OF LANGUAGE

Golding uses a flashback – Ralph pondering on his previous existence in Devonport – to create a further contrast between life on the island and the boys' previous lives.

Golding also uses carefully chosen words such as 'uncompromising', 'impossible' and 'sheer' (p. 128) to suggest the boys' isolation. This word choice now gives the impression that the island is a prison rather than a paradise like that in *The Coral Island*.

As you read through this chapter, notice how Golding further implies that the island is a hostile place.

Remember to mention the linguistic devices and figurative language used – such as similes and metaphors and their effects.

> **TOP TIP** **A01**
>
> Notice how some of the themes are developed in this chapter. They include crowd mentality, civilisation versus savagery and the qualities needed for leadership.

CHAPTER EIGHT: GIFT FOR THE DARKNESS

SUMMARY

- Ralph, Jack and Roger report what they have seen. Jack argues that the hunters can kill the beast.
- Ralph describes the hunters as 'Boys armed with sticks' (p. 137), which hurts Jack.
- Jack tries to overthrow Ralph as leader but he is rejected as the new chief and he leaves, soon to be joined by most of the older boys.
- A fire is relit by the platform.
- Jack goes off with his hunters to kill pigs. They kill a sow who has piglets and decide to invite the others to a feast in order to steal their fire.
- They sever the sow's head and put it on a stick.
- Simon, alone in the forest, sees the pig's head and has a 'conversation' with it, before losing consciousness.

CHECKPOINT 12 **A01**

What are Piggy's feelings when Jack departs?

WHY IS THIS CHAPTER IMPORTANT?

A It shows just how much Jack **hates** Ralph.

B Golding highlights Ralph and Piggy's **realistic approach** when they concede that the boys would be **powerless** against a beast.

C The chapter signals the **split** of the **survivors** into two groups: the **conch group** and the **hunters**. This is a natural development of the differences between the two main characters.

D There is further evidence that Jack's style of leadership is a descent into the **primitive**. Debate and discussion are replaced by rehearsed and ritualised responses: 'The Chief has spoken' (p. 155).

E We witness Simon's strange behaviour when he communicates with the 'Lord of the Flies' (p. 157), but we also see a **courageous** side to his character.

KEY CHARACTER: JACK AS A LEADER

Golding clarifies Jack's leadership style in this chapter, showing how he wants to be in charge to please his own ego. He craves power for himself and does not take responsibility for others in the way that Ralph does.

Piggy recognises Jack's focus on his ego, telling Ralph, 'Now you done it. You been rude about his hunters' (p. 137). Piggy sees that it is dangerous to insult Jack's tribe.

Jack blows the conch for the first time to call an assembly. He conforms to law and order but intends to use it to his advantage. When questioned, he shouts, 'Quiet!' and 'You listen' (p. 138), signs that debate will not be permitted. Jack informs his hunters that he's 'going to be chief' (p. 146) and he becomes an authoritarian leader, making it clear that those who disobey will be punished.

Jack uses the fear of a beast to his own advantage. This is why he offers the pig's head as a gift. The possible existence of a beast gives a new importance to Jack's hunters. They are now defending the boys.

KEY CONTEXT: LORD OF THE FLIES

Golding chose this phrase as the book's title to emphasise the themes of good/evil and civilisation/savagery in the novel, as it relates to both savagery and evil.

There are references in ancient history to a 'god of the flies' being worshipped by pagan civilisations. Although Jack has said that they are going to forget about the beast, the pig's head is still left as a gift. This can be seen as symbolic since primitive man left offerings to pagan gods. Jack's tribe has become primitive.

There is acceptance of, and respect for, this unnamed being raised to the status of a god. There is a parallel between the way the boys refer to their 'god' – the Lord of the Flies – and the way that they idolise Jack, who is, in a sense, lord over them – his own flies, or menials.

AIMING HIGH: DISCUSS WHAT CHARACTERS REPRESENT

Lord of the Flies is famously an allegory, in which events and people represent various ideas. To demonstrate higher levels of analysis, it is useful to be able to show how Golding has created different layers of allegory. For example, some critics have identified a psychological allegory based on Freud's ideas, in which the three main characters, Ralph, Piggy and Jack, represent the three key aspects of the self.

Jack's association with the id – the primal, instinctive part of us – is clear early on and developed in this chapter as he takes other boys with him to 'hunt and feast and have fun' (p. 154). Piggy's role is the superego – the part that sets limits and seeks to control the id's impulses because of morality – while Ralph represents the ego – the part which follows society's rules and balances the id and the superego. Commenting on this as well as the idea of religious or political allegory will allow you to demonstrate a more complex appreciation of the novel.

TOP TIP **A01**

Think about changes in mood. There are two periods of optimism – when the boys are first on the island and when Jack leaves. Both periods of optimism are destroyed by Jack.

CHECKPOINT 13 **A01**

What does the voice of a schoolmaster used by the Lord of the Flies represent?

KEY CONTEXT **A03**

In the Bible, one of the Devil's names is Be'elzebub, which translates as 'Lord of the Flies'. As well as pagan associations, the name is clearly connected with the idea of evil.

CHECKPOINT 14 **A01**

In what ways does Piggy behave like a parent?

TOP TIP **A02**

Images of light and dark, clear and opaque, are important throughout the book but are particularly strong in this chapter. They could represent the good and evil in the boys' minds or the good and evil existing on the island. In this chapter the storm corresponds to the boys' moods (pathetic fallacy).

CHECKPOINT 15 **A01**

Some critics have seen Simon as a prophet or as a Christ-like figure. What do you think?

TOP TIP **A02**

When the mob is in action, the weather is often in sympathy with the victim (pathetic fallacy). An example is when Simon is mistaken for the beast and killed – 'Then the clouds opened and let down the rain like a waterfall' (Ch. 9, p. 169).

KEY CONTEXT **A03**

Golding was a Christian, so it is appropriate to interpret his presentation of Simon as a Christ-figure who dies for the others. How does Simon's death benefit the other boys? Does it benefit all the boys in the same way?

CHAPTER NINE: A VIEW TO A DEATH

SUMMARY

- Simon sees the dead parachutist and discovers the truth about the beast. He heads off to tell the others.
- Ralph and Piggy join Jack's party, where they are eating meat and having a feast.
- Jack asks who will join his tribe and he and Ralph argue over where the conch can be used.
- A thunderstorm starts and Piggy senses trouble.
- Jack encourages his tribe to do their dance.
- Simon stumbles into the dancing circle.
- The boys see Simon as the beast and kill him in a frenzied attack.
- The bodies of Simon and the parachutist are washed out to sea.

WHY IS THIS CHAPTER IMPORTANT?

A It shows the **contrast** between both Jack's camp and the earlier assemblies, and Jack and Ralph's leadership styles.

B Simon discovers the **truth** concerning the beast but is unable to bring the truth to the others.

C Simon's death marks a **change** in the hunters' **attitude** towards **death**. It also allows Jack to play on the boys' fears.

D The death also brings about a **burden of guilt** as all took part in the murder.

E Golding uses **nature**, **colour** and imagery to effect in the chapter.

F The **disappearance** of the **parachutist's body** is a convenient **plot device**, as it removes the possibility that it will be discovered and revealed for what it is.

KEY CHARACTER: SIMON – THE MARTYR FOR THE TRUTH

Golding develops the characterisation of Simon as a Christ-like figure most obviously in this chapter. Simon is determined to reach the top of the mountain, where the truth lies – both literally and metaphorically. Simon frees the dead airman, who is then given the dignity of a burial at sea. Simon, too, is consigned to the sea after his murder.

The news of 'a body on the hill' (p. 169) provides a clear piece of Christian imagery. Simon can be viewed as a prophet and visionary, with a parallel between the parachutist on the mountain and Christ crucified on the hill at Calvary. The description of the halo of creatures that surround him with light as he floats out to sea is both poignant and significant.

KEY QUOTATION: SIMON AS 'THE BEAST'   **A02**

Golding shifts from writing about Simon to calling him a 'thing' and then 'the beast' on p. 168, so that we see Simon clearly through the boys' eyes. This use of narrative perspective makes it easier for us to understand the point of view of the mob: 'The beast was on its knees in the centre, its arms folded over its face.' (p. 168) Golding creates distance between the reader and Simon at this point, just as the boys are unable at that moment to see him as human.

CHECKPOINT 16   A01

What fate do Simon and the parachutist share?

EXAM FOCUS: WRITING ABOUT EFFECTS   **A02**

Golding's language choices in his descriptions are usually worth commenting on when you are writing about effects. Read this example by one student focusing on nature and colour leading up to Simon's death:

Clear focus on Golding's purpose and intention

Golding uses detailed description of bad weather coming onto the island to begin the build up to Simon's death. He shows how nature becomes colourless, as colours 'drained from water and trees', contrasting this with the pig's guts, which look like a heap of glistening coal'. The blood that 'gushed out' from Simon's nose would be red, adding another contrast to colourless nature and perhaps foreshadowing the violence to come, as the storm reaches the island.

Useful application of terminology showing Golding's intended effect

Before the violence builds, Golding shows how Ralph notices the flames against the 'dull light'. When evening arrives, he sees it is 'not with calm beauty but with the threat of violence'. When lightning strikes, it is described as a 'blue-white scar', implying it has torn or injured the sky.

Good choice of quotation analysed effectively for implied meaning

Clear sense of effect of the descriptions

Golding has cleverly used nature as a hostile force to contribute to the atmosphere of confusion and fear. When the boys see Simon, it is through flashes of lightning and in the dark (almost like a strobe-light effect).

Now you try it:

The last paragraph needs another sentence or two to complete it. Add one which evaluates the build-up to Simon's death. How do you think this atmosphere helps to make the killing more realistic?

CHAPTER TEN: THE SHELL AND THE GLASSES

SUMMARY

- Piggy and Ralph talk about the events of the previous night.
- Sam and Eric join them. Guilt-ridden, the four boys lie to each other about their involvement.
- Jack and his hunters set up camp at the far end of the island.
- Roger is challenged on returning to Jack's camp and admires the lever and rock device ready to prevent unwelcome visitors.
- Ralph, Piggy and the twins try, unsuccessfully, to relight the fire. Ralph shows signs of confusion and they give up on the fire for the evening.
- In their shelters that night, they hear noises outside.
- Jack and two of his hunters attack and steal Piggy's glasses.
- Jack is delighted at his achievement – 'He was a chief now in truth' (p. 186).

TOP TIP (A01)

Ralph and Eric, by accident, fight each other in the darkness. Could this symbolise the pointlessness of violence – used without thought or reason?

WHY IS THIS CHAPTER IMPORTANT?

A We witness **discussions** about Simon's death, which Piggy insists was an **accident**.

B Now that Jack has become **chief** we understand that he has **unchecked powers**.

C When one of the boys, Wilfred, is punished for some undisclosed offence, this demonstrates Jack's **authoritarian** leadership.

D Golding shows how Jack is revered and set apart as important in his camp, where he is chief. This **contrasts** sharply with the assemblies, where everyone was considered of **equal value**. Roger – always the cruellest boy – praises Jack as a 'proper Chief' (p. 176).

E We learn how the hunters, under Jack's leadership, are willing to use **violence** to obtain what they want – in this case, Piggy's glasses.

KEY CHARACTERS: THE TWO GROUPS (A02)

Golding creates an atmosphere of hopelessness and gloom among both the conch group and the savages of Castle Rock following Simon's murder. Interestingly, both groups are unable to accept full responsibility for what they have done.

Golding uses these denials to show how the two groups work. The conch group are able to work together and support each other. None of them can face the enormity of what has happened, but Golding uses repetition, making them echo each other's words to show how well they work as a unit: 'we were very tired' (p. 175). The Castle Rock group, however, take far less time to conclude 'How could we – kill – it?' (p. 177), operating at a simpler – more primitive – level with less discussion and no real cooperation. Jack says they didn't kill it, and that is that.

The two groups represent civilisation and savagery, something else that Golding emphasises through their language in these denials. It is significant that the Castle Rock group never utter the name Simon, but seem to be talking about the beast who 'came – disguised' (p. 177). The conch group, on the other hand, accept what happened, and that it happened to Simon, but cannot accept their part in it. The savage group can readily accept the chase and the kill, but the civilised group cannot deny that it was a person in the middle of the mob and not the beast.

KEY LANGUAGE: THE SHELL AND THE GLASSES AS SYMBOLS (A02)

Golding named this chapter 'The Shell and the Glasses', both of which are symbols. The shell could represent democracy, the voice of reason or decency. It is of no use in itself beyond being a beautiful object – its use lies in what it represents or symbolises to the boys.

The glasses are useful to Piggy, but have a function beyond that for everyone else – they can start a fire. The ability to make fire is something that sets human beings apart from animals. The glasses, therefore, symbolise not only fire, but also knowledge – enlightenment – and mastery over primitive instincts.

Note that Piggy perceives the conch as the more valuable item, holding it – literally – with respect and affection during the events of the next chapter.

TOP TIP: WRITING ABOUT JACK'S LEADERSHIP IN CONTEXT (A03)

Look at how both Jack and the boys are referred to in order to link Jack's leadership to the context Golding was writing in. Jack is not named, only called 'the Chief' (p. 176), while the rest of the boys are simply 'the tribe' (p. 176) or 'the savages' (p. 177). In the dictatorships of the 1930s and 1940s, enigmatic leaders such as Hitler, Mussolini and Stalin were revered initially, while the people they led faced loss of individuality and strict discipline.

CHECKPOINT 17 (A01)

How does Piggy avoid his feelings of guilt for the death of Simon?

TOP TIP (A01)

Does Jack believe in the beast or is he using fear as a method of control? What do **you** think?

CHECKPOINT 18 (A01)

How does Jack conduct his meetings?

CHAPTER ELEVEN: CASTLE ROCK

SUMMARY

- Ralph is unable to light the fire without Piggy's glasses.
- The conch group decide to confront Jack and his hunters.
- A scuffle breaks out between the two groups at Castle Rock.
- Roger leans on the lever, which catapults a heavy rock towards Piggy.
- Piggy is killed by the falling rock and the conch is destroyed.
- Sam and Eric are captured by the hunters.
- Ralph is now alone, forced to escape as hunters hurl spears in his direction.

WHY IS THIS CHAPTER IMPORTANT?

A Despite Jack's **crimes**, we see that Ralph intends to approach him as a **civilised human being** and explain the seriousness of the situation.

B Piggy's faith in the ultimate **power** of the **conch** is exhibited when he proudly carries the shell to Castle Rock.

C It is evident that **Sam** and **Eric** are forced to join **Jack's savages** through **violent coercion** rather than **reason**; the rule of law is coming to an end.

D When the conch is shattered and Piggy is killed, both the symbol of **civilised behaviour** and the **voice of reason** are destroyed.

E Golding shows us how Ralph, with the rest of his group gone, copes with being the **sole target** of the others' hatred.

TOP TIP (A01)

Look at the last remnants of civilisation in this chapter: Ralph and Piggy are still hoping the symbols of order will help them.

TOP TIP (A01)

Sam and Eric are often seen as representing the mass population in the novel's political allegory. Their similarity to each other could also be seen as evidence of this. As 'little people', their individuality is insignificant to the political system as a whole.

KEY CONTEXT: CHILDREN'S LITERATURE IN THE 1940S AND 1950S (A03)

Golding uses some of the conventions of a series of children's books about Billy Bunter to help the contemporary audience see Piggy as a type of joke figure at the start of the novel. Billy Bunter was a comic fictitious public schoolboy who liked his food and had a superior attitude to the other boys. The first Bunter story (which evolved from earlier comic stories) was published in 1947 by Frank Richards. The stories were so popular that a TV series about Billy Bunter's exploits at Greyfriars School emerged in the 1950s. Readers of *Lord of the Flies* in the 1960s would have identified Piggy as a Billy Bunter type, and therefore seen him as a figure of fun and perhaps felt sympathetic towards him.

KEY CHARACTER: THE DEATH OF PIGGY (A02)

There is a clear parallel between the death of the pigs and the death of Piggy. Look at Piggy's demise – 'arms and legs twitched a bit, like a pig's after it has been killed' (p. 201) – and note the similarities with the graphic earlier accounts of pig killings (in Chapter 8, for example).

The focus on Piggy as 'the centre of social derision' (Ch. 9, p. 165) – a source of amusement – ends. Previously, the humour had been caused by:

● Slapstick (boys falling off the 'twister' log – Ch. 5, p. 82 – at the assembly)

● Pantomime mimicry (Maurice pretending to be the pig – Ch. 4, p. 79)

● The Billy-Bunter-like earnestness of Piggy ('the tribe were curious to hear what amusing thing he might have to say' – Ch. 11, p. 199)

Schoolboy humour, or indeed fun of any sort, is not seen after Piggy's death.

CHECKPOINT 19 (A01)

What, says Piggy, is the one thing Jack hasn't got?

TOP TIP (A02)

What is Piggy's significance to the novel as a whole? Think particularly about what he symbolises and which themes he is associated with. How would the novel be different without him?

KEY QUOTATION: ORDER VERSUS CHAOS (A02)

This key theme is expressed clearly by Ralph when he asks 'the savages', 'Which is better – to have rules and agree, or to hunt and kill?' (p. 200) Asking this question at this point shows Ralph's optimism and emphasises how important this theme is to Golding. Ralph has to shout his question over the noise that Jack's tribe are making, but as Golding's symbol of civilisation and order, this is the crucial point that he needs to make at this time.

KEY THEME: AN INCREASE IN VIOLENCE (A01)

Golding's knowledge of schoolboys from his teaching days is clear in how he uses the idea of play and games. Play is a prominent form of behaviour and is evident when the boys are first on the island. In nature, play is often practice for something else – play fighting prepares animals for hunting, for example. In human beings, it may develop beyond the need for survival into more sophisticated social skills.

At this point, Roger's stone throwing becomes dangerous and Jack's exaggerated dominance in the 'game' becomes sinister. When Piggy is killed and the conch destroyed, Jack has no remorse, declaring boldly to Ralph, 'There isn't a tribe for you any more!'(p. 201). He adds, significantly, 'The conch is gone—' (p. 201). The old rules are over; childhood innocence is lost.

When Jack hurls his spear at Ralph, 'Viciously, with full intention' (p. 201), this is no game. He clearly means to wound Ralph, who represents the opposition.

TOP TIP (A03)

When referring to context (such as Golding's teaching experience), make sure you can relate it to the text, as specifically as possible. You will not get credit for just knowing about Golding's life – your task is to use this to help you analyse the novel.

TOP TIP: WRITING ABOUT THE RULE OF ORDER (A02)

The ideal of civilisation and order persists within the conch group to the bitter end. This can be demonstrated when Samneric are captured and Sam protests 'out of the heart of civilisation' with the stereotypically English exclamation 'Oh, I say!' (p. 198). Just as Piggy has faith in the conch to the end, so the other boys in favour of order cling to patterns of civilised behaviour, even in the face of violence and chaos.

AIMING HIGH: COMMENT ON DIFFERENT POSSIBILITIES ⭐

It is worth discussing what Piggy represents, but if you really want to demonstrate a subtle awareness, offer more than one possibility. He is usually described as symbolising civilisation, or order because of his faith in the conch and his strong sense of fair play. He also represents logic and clear-sightedness, and could be said to represent the adult viewpoint: he has been brought up by his aunt and appears to have the foresight and good sense of an older person, together with a degree of caution and some organising ability. A subtle and detailed exploration of Piggy's character should be able to consider more than one interpretation.

CHAPTER TWELVE: CRY OF THE HUNTERS

SUMMARY

- Ralph considers his options as he tries to hide and avoid danger.
- He encounters the pig's head and experiences fear and anger, lashing out at it and taking away the spear that supported it.
- Ralph goes to speak to Sam and Eric at Castle Rock, but their manner is discouraging. They tell him that Roger has 'sharpened a stick at both ends' (p. 211).
- Ralph becomes aware that he is totally alone.
- Jack and the hunters track Ralph as if he were an animal.
- Jack sets most of the island on fire to smoke Ralph out.
- The smoke from the fire is seen by a passing ship.
- Ralph, exhausted, collapses on the beach. He looks up to see the friendly face of a rescuing naval officer.

CHECKPOINT 20 **A01**

What might the pig's head represent for Ralph?

WHY IS THIS CHAPTER IMPORTANT?

A As Ralph **spies** on Castle Rock, we appreciate how hard it is for him to come to terms with **all that has happened**.

B When Ralph sees the remains of the **pig's head** we are reminded of **Simon's** earlier, very different reaction to the object.

C Ralph fails to see the significance of the sharpened stick, but we realise that he will be **hunted** like a pig.

D When rescuing the boys, the naval officer sees Jack as a **little boy**, rather than seeing his primitive, underlying aggression and savagery.

E Golding makes it clear that it is only **external intervention** that saves Ralph from certain death.

KEY CHARACTERS: ROGER AND THE SAVAGES (A01)

Golding shows more than the loss of civilisation in this chapter – he shows the boys actively seeking to destroy it through hunting Ralph, the last representative of order on the island. Roger has become sadistic, Sam and Eric calling him 'a terror' (p. 210). He is prepared to kill and behead Ralph, and place Ralph's head on the stick instead of a pig's head. This is why the stick is sharpened 'at both ends' (p. 211).

The hunters are now clearly savages. The savages will sweep across the island in line to catch Ralph – communicating (like primitive man) with wavering cries. They lever one of the rocks on the cliff top and it crashes into the thicket, missing him. The savages cheer as it falls – having lost all their humanity.

Under Jack's direction, the savages set the forest on fire with the aim of smoking Ralph out. The raging fire burns the fruit trees – a valuable food source. The boys' inability to plan for the future is part of their savagery.

TOP TIP (A02)

Readers are given 'insight' into events that the characters do not always have. This is called **dramatic irony**. How can you tell that Ralph does not appreciate the danger he is in?

KEY CHARACTER: RALPH'S RESCUE (A02)

Ralph, the only boy left who has some vestiges of civilised behaviour, can hear the tribal dancing and see savages keeping lookout. He regrets his isolation and discovers that Jack intends to hunt him like a pig. As he heads towards the forest, the cries of the hunters sweep the island behind him.

It is ironic that the smoke and fire made to flush out Ralph is the boys' means of rescue. Presumably, if rescue had not come, Ralph would have been murdered and the island would have been destroyed by fire.

KEY QUOTATION: THE BOYS AND THE OUTSIDE WORLD (A02)

The naval officer's questions to Ralph demonstrate his inability to understand what has been going on. He treats the hunt like a game initially: 'What have you been doing? Having a war or something?' (p. 223), showing his assumption that the boys are still like innocent children in a playground. Golding's use of irony here makes the ending more poignant.

TOP TIP: WRITING ABOUT NATURE (A02)

Notice how Ralph was 'scratched and bruised from his flight through the forest' (p. 203), showing how nature has injured him. He was unable to bathe his wounds, as he would not feel safe from Jack's tribe 'by the little stream or on the open beach' (p. 203) – nature also failed to offer him any help.

In the final chapter, light and dark are used to describe the trees and foliage. This could represent the good and bad that Golding wanted to emphasise is present in us all.

PROGRESS AND REVISION CHECK

SECTION ONE: CHECK YOUR KNOWLEDGE

Answer these quick questions to test your basic knowledge of the novel, its characters and events:

1. Why are the boys on the island?

2. What is described here responding to Ralph's first conch call: 'something dark was fumbling along [the beach]' (p. 15)?

3. Where is the signal fire lit?

4. All the boys build the first shelter together, but most of them get bored of building and wander off. Who helps Ralph and Piggy build the last shelter?

5. What does Jack use to change his appearance?

6. Something makes Ralph change his attitude towards Piggy. What does Ralph say that Piggy can do in Chapter 5?

7. Who is silenced in the meeting when he tries to make the boys realise 'maybe [the beast is] only us' (p. 96)?

8. Which of the bigger boys stays behind to look after the littluns when the beast is hunted?

9. Who is hurt when the boys re-enact their hunt in Chapter 7?

10. Who reminisces in Chapter 7 about eating 'cornflakes with sugar and cream' and about the books which were 'dog-eared and scratched' (p. 123)?

11. What is the 'Gift for the Darkness', given to the beast in Chapter 8?

12. What claims to be the reason 'things are what they are' (p. 158), speaking to Simon in the forest?

13. What natural event occurs in Chapter 9, adding to the atmosphere and lead-up to Simon's death?

14. What is Simon trying to tell the others when he runs into the frenzied mob?

15. What does Piggy insist Simon's death was?

16. Who does Ralph fight with in the dark when Jack's group attack?

17. Ralph and his group decide to confront Jack's group in Chapter 11. What is it that they need from them?

18. What is smashed along with Piggy?

19. Who warns Ralph that Roger has 'sharpened a stick at both ends' (p. 211)?

20. Why is the naval officer 'moved and a little embarrassed' (p. 225) at the very end of the novel?

PROGRESS AND REVISION CHECK

SECTION TWO: CHECK YOUR UNDERSTANDING

Here are two tasks on the significance of particular moments in the novel. These require more thought and slightly longer responses. In each case, try to write at least three to four paragraphs.

Task 1: In Chapter 4, pp. 65–7, in what ways is the section in which Jack paints his face significant? Think about:

- How it relates to the idea of savagery
- What we learn about his character

Task 2: At the end of Chapter 8, pp. 157–9, why is the section in which Simon talks to the pig's head important? Think about:

- What we learn about Simon's position on the island
- How Golding uses language to emphasise the idea of evil

PROGRESS CHECK

GOOD PROGRESS

I can:

- Understand how Golding has sequenced and revealed events. ☐
- Refer to the importance of key events in the novel. ☐
- Select well-chosen evidence, including key quotations, to support my ideas. ☐

EXCELLENT PROGRESS

I can:

- Refer in depth to main and minor events and how they contribute to the development of the plot. ☐
- Understand how Golding has carefully ordered or revealed events for particular effects. ☐
- Draw on a range of carefully selected key evidence, including quotations, to support my ideas. ☐

WHO'S WHO?

ROGER

JACK

RALPH

PIGGY

MAURICE

SAM N ERIC

SIMON

BIGUNS

PERCIVAL

JOHNNY

LITTLUNS

RALPH

RALPH'S ROLE IN THE NOVEL

Ralph is the chief and uses the conch to control meetings. He has the responsibility of looking after the other survivors. In the novel he:

- blows the conch to summon other survivors (see Ch. 1, pp. 12–13)
- decides to build a fire to help the boys get rescued (see Ch. 2, p. 37)
- attempts to build shelters for the younger boys (see Ch. 3, p. 50)
- raises issues to aid survival and rescue (see Ch. 5, pp. 84–8)
- shows courage, exploring a part of the island where the other boys think the beast may lurk (see Ch. 6, pp. 114–15)
- is hunted by the savages and saved by the naval officer (see Ch. 12, p. 222).

RALPH'S IMPORTANCE TO THE NOVEL AS A WHOLE

As the first character we meet, then elected chief, Ralph is the novel's protagonist. He represents order and civilisation and Golding uses him to show a practical and rational approach to the problems that face the boys.

Ralph is an easy character to sympathise with, as he seems ordinary (having none of Simon's strangeness or Piggy's social difficulties, for example) and reasonable. Furthermore, Golding makes him a sympathetic character because it is usually Ralph's view that is presented sympathetically in the novel. This shows that Golding views him as admirable.

At the end of the novel, Ralph is perhaps the least changed boy left, having not given in to savagery. He is the only one to communicate at all coherently with the naval officer.

TOP TIP (A02)

It is significant that Ralph notices the conch and insists on the need for signal fires, as both of these elements are linked to the idea of civilisation.

TOP TIP: WRITING ABOUT RALPH AND PIGGY'S RELATIONSHIP **(A01)**

When you are writing about Ralph and Piggy's relationship, make sure that you track how Golding uses this to show changes in Ralph throughout the novel. Remember that although Ralph is dismissive of Piggy at the start of the novel, he does not possess Jack's malice. Having upset Piggy by using his nickname to raise a laugh, he appreciates Piggy's sense of humiliation and finds a way out: 'Better Piggy than Fatty ... I'm sorry if you feel like that' (Ch. 1, pp. 21–2). This apology shows that he is able to act diplomatically, demonstrating his leadership abilities in handling other people's feelings. Through listening to Piggy, Ralph learns to take his responsibilities seriously – thinking of rescue and shelter.

KEY CONTEXT **(A03)**

One possible way of viewing the text is as a struggle between democratic and totalitarian forces (represented in Golding's day by the West – the USA, UK, etc. – and the USSR, now Russia).

EXAM FOCUS: WRITING ABOUT RALPH **(A01)**

Key point	Evidence/Further meaning
• Ralph has no hidden depths or unhealthy character traits.	• 'there was a mildness about his mouth and eyes that proclaimed no devil.' (Ch. 1, p. 5) • Suggests that Ralph is gentle and can be trusted, as he is exactly what he seems.
• Ralph's efforts are directed to keeping the fire going.	• 'They'll see our smoke.' (Ch. 4, p. 69) • Shows Ralph's focus on practical matters, and his ability to plan for longer-term goals.
• Ralph listens to Piggy's advice.	• 'new understanding that Piggy had given him.' (Ch. 7, p. 129) • Reveals Ralph's awareness that Piggy's thinking skills are superior and have helped him lead effectively.
• Only Ralph is able to come to terms with the reasons why Simon was killed.	• 'Don't you understand, Piggy? The things we did—' (Ch. 10, p. 173) • Shows his true leadership qualities. He is willing to share the blame and responsibility for Simon's death.

REVISION FOCUS: RALPH

Try making a list of Ralph's qualities. For example, Ralph is:

- Able to see the good in people and in the island
- Easy to like and naturally at ease
- Tall, blond, good-looking and one of the older boys
- Able to speak at meetings and considers other people
- A natural leader

Find up to three quotations from different parts of the novel to show each of these qualities.

JACK

JACK'S ROLE IN THE NOVEL

Jack is leader of the choirboys, who become his hunters. He is a rival to Ralph and eventually declares himself as chief. In the novel he:

- decides the choir will be hunters (see Ch. 1, p. 19)
- snatches Piggy's glasses to make a fire (see Ch. 2, p. 40)
- kills a pig and organises a chant and dance to celebrate the pig's death (see Ch. 4, p. 72)
- has a disregard for rules (see Ch. 5, p. 99)
- runs off when Ralph is re-elected as chief (see Ch. 8, pp. 139–40)
- becomes a cruel leader of his tribe (see Ch. 11, p. 201).

TOP TIP (A02)

Physical descriptions are only worth mentioning in written responses if they add to the understanding of character or behaviour. Jack's physical description is a deliberate warning sign. His red hair stands out. As well as often being associated with a fiery temper, it perhaps also indicates danger.

JACK'S IMPORTANCE TO THE NOVEL AS A WHOLE

Jack is the novel's **antagonist**, representing chaos and savagery. His behaviour is directed by his desire to hunt and he is unable to plan for the future, being unconcerned about long-term needs such as shelter and trying to be rescued. His links to savagery can be seen by his strong association with the mask, the chant and the primitive act of offering the sow's head to the beast.

Golding rarely presents Jack in a sympathetic light, suggesting that he wants the reader to judge him and, more important, what he represents in a negative way. Jack's cruelty towards Piggy, his arrogance from the beginning and his inability to think beyond his immediate desires make him both a poor leader and an unsympathetic character.

EXAM FOCUS: WRITING ABOUT JACK (A01)

Key point	Evidence/Further meaning
• Jack is someone who does not want to obey.	• 'This was the voice of one who knew his own mind.' (Ch. 1, p. 17) • Suggests that he is certain of his own ideas and is not willing to compromise.
• Jack has an almost addictive urge to kill.	• Jack had a 'compulsion to track down and kill that was swallowing him up.' (Ch. 3, p. 51) • Shows that he represents Man the Hunter and exhibits a basic, primeval instinct to hunt.
• Jack turns from hunting pigs to hunting people.	• 'Do our dance! Come on! Dance!' (Ch. 9, p. 167) • Reveals that he is the one who sets in motion the sequence of events that lead to Simon's death.
• When painted, Jack feels he can act as he wishes.	• 'the mask was a thing on its own, behind which Jack hid, liberated from shame and self-consciousness.' (Ch. 4, p. 66) • Makes the mask sound responsible, as though it makes him act in an extreme or evil way.

TOP TIP: WRITING ABOUT JACK (A01)

Make sure you understand how Golding has presented Jack as unlikeable. He is not only personally unpleasant, but also not practical. His overwhelming hunting instinct is both self-destructive and lacking in foresight, leading to at least one lost chance of rescue.

There are various key moments that you could explore to demonstrate Golding's negative presentation of him, for example:

- His dramatic entrance (Ch. 1, pp. 15–16)
- His constant dismissal of Piggy
- His failure to maintain the signal fire (Ch. 4, pp. 69–76)
- The boys killing the sow, which could have bred and provided future meat (Ch. 8, pp. 148–9)
- The boys destroying the fruit trees (Ch. 12, p. 220).

TOP TIP (A02)

Notice how Jack is portrayed as at the mercy of his desires: he has a 'compulsion' (Ch. 3, p. 51) to hunt and is 'liberated' (Ch. 4, p. 66) from civilised feelings by the mask.

PIGGY

PIGGY'S ROLE IN THE NOVEL

Piggy is overweight, concerned about his health and does not like manual labour. Unlike Ralph, Jack and the choirboys, he is clearly working class. Piggy is arguably the most intelligent boy on the island. In the novel he:

- is the first boy to meet Ralph (see Ch. 1, p. 1)
- is the first to suggest he and Ralph have 'to do something' (see Ch. 1, p. 10)
- suggests the conch is used to 'call the others' and 'Have a meeting' (see Ch. 1, p. 12)
- suggests the only fear on the island should be the fear 'of people' (see Ch. 5, p. 90)
- tells Ralph he will carry the conch to Castle Rock and confront Jack (see Ch. 11, p. 189)
- is killed by a giant rock released by Roger (see Ch. 11, pp. 200–1).

EXAM FOCUS: WRITING ABOUT PIGGY (A01)

Key point	Evidence/Further meaning
• Piggy's size sets him apart from the other boys and makes him different.	• 'He was shorter than the fair boy and very fat.' (Ch. 1, p.1) • Shows how Golding emphasises his physical difference from the very start.
• Piggy is an outsider who is immediately loathed and bullied by Jack.	• 'Piggy was an outsider, not only by accent, which did not matter, but by fat, and ass-mar, and specs, and a certain disinclination for manual labour' (Ch. 4, p. 68) • Shows that Piggy appears to have little in his favour when survival on a desert island is at stake.
• Piggy is intelligent.	• 'them that haven't no common sense' (Ch. 8, p. 145) • Shows how he is able to see to the heart of the matter – he is **metaphorically**, if not literally, clear sighted.
• Piggy can solve problems using rational thought.	• 'We could find out how to make a small hot fire and then put green branches on to make smoke.' (Ch. 8, p. 143) • Shows him making suggestions and working collaboratively.

SIMON

SIMON'S ROLE IN THE NOVEL

Simon enters the novel as one of Jack's choirboys. He faints and is often referred to as strange. He is the only boy who discovers the truth about the beast. In the novel he:

- faints as Jack leads his choir along the beach (see Ch. 1, p. 16)
- joins Ralph and Jack to explore parts of the island (see Ch. 1, p. 20)
- goes off alone into the jungle (see Ch. 3, p. 56)
- gives his piece of meat to Piggy (see Ch. 4, p. 78)
- 'communicates' with the 'Lord of the Flies' and loses consciousness (see Ch. 8, pp. 157–9)
- discovers the dead parachutist and is killed when he comes to tell the boys the truth about the beast (see Ch. 9, pp. 161–2, 168–9).

EXAM FOCUS: WRITING ABOUT SIMON

Key point	Evidence/Further meaning
● Simon is seen by the others as strange in an unspecified way.	● 'batty', 'queer', 'funny', 'cracked' ● These adjectives show the boys' lack of vocabulary to define him.
● Simon is unable to explain the notion of evil, which manifests itself in the idea of the fear and the beast.	● 'What's the dirtiest thing there is?' (Ch. 5, p. 96) ● Shows that, although he has the intelligence and maturity to understand the concept, he lacks the necessary language skills to express it.
● Simon understands the nature of the beast (the dead parachutist).	● 'The beast was harmless and horrible.' (Ch. 9, p. 162) ● He understands the implications for the boys: that there is nothing to fear and there is life beyond the island.
● Simon has considerable strength of mind but his body is frail.	● 'In Simon's right temple, a pulse began to beat on the brain.' (Ch. 8, p. 152) ● Shows his perceptiveness and individuality but also his vulnerability.

TOP TIP: WRITING ABOUT SIMON (A02)

Golding presents Simon as ever-present – Simon is described by Jack as 'always about' (Ch. 3, p. 56). He is loyal and is the only boy who helps Ralph with the third shelter. However, he also spends time alone and seems to be the only boy who regularly seeks this. Simon is often regarded by critics as a prophet – even a saint or Christ-like figure. He is the one who confronts the Lord of the Flies, who symbolises Jack's evil. He is murdered bringing the truth back to the other boys. Had he lived to tell them the truth, he would have destroyed Jack's power.

ROGER AND MAURICE

ROGER AND MAURICE'S ROLES IN THE NOVEL

Roger is Jack's lieutenant. He has a sadistic streak. Maurice is Roger's henchman.

- Roger and Maurice are part of Jack's choir (see Ch. 1, p. 18).
- Roger and Maurice destroy the littluns' sandcastles and kick sand in Percival's eye (see Ch. 4, p. 62).
- Roger, concealed by a tree, teases a littlun by throwing stones aimed to land close by (see Ch. 4, pp. 64–5).
- Roger is the first person Jack shows the mask clay to (see Ch. 4, p. 65).
- Roger acts 'with a sense of delirious abandonment' when he brings about Piggy's death (see Ch. 11, p. 200).
- Roger has a stick sharpened 'at both ends' when the boys hunt Ralph (see Ch. 12, p. 211).

EXAM FOCUS: WRITING ABOUT ROGER AND MAURICE (A01)

Key point	Evidence/Further meaning
• Roger is the boy who most obviously turns from choirboy into pre-meditated killer.	• 'You don't know Roger. He's a terror.' (Ch. 12, p. 210) • Shows that he outstrips even Jack in barbarism, as the twins comment first on Roger, then 'the Chief'.
• When Roger and Maurice kick sand in Percival's eye, Maurice feels guilty.	• 'Maurice still felt the unease of wrong-doing.' (Ch. 4, p. 63) • Shows that he retains a sense of sin.
• Roger is the person who administers torture.	• 'Roger advanced upon them as one wielding a nameless authority.' (Ch. 11, p. 202) • Reveals that he appears to enjoy his role and will be backed up by Jack.
• Roger shows no remorse for the death of Piggy and is willing to kill Ralph.	• Samneric say that the Chief and Roger are both '"–terrors" "–only Roger–"' (Ch. 12, p. 210) • Suggests that Roger will go further than Jack.

TOP TIP: WRITING ABOUT ROGER AND MAURICE (A01)

It is easy to underestimate Roger's role in the novel, but contrasting him with Maurice can help to make it clearer. While Golding clearly shows both observing 'the taboo of the old life' against direct violence early in the novel (Ch. 4, p. 65), Roger's descent into savagery and active cruelty is made clear. Maurice, however, remains relatively unchanged: once a loyal choirboy, he becomes a loyal follower of Jack and Roger.

SAM AND ERIC

SAM AND ERIC'S ROLE IN THE NOVEL

Sam and Eric are twins who do everything together. When they first appear, they are described as boys who 'breathed together' and 'grinned together' (Ch. 1, p. 15). In the novel Sam and Eric:

- look after the fire but fall asleep and almost let it out (see Ch. 6, p. 104)
- believe the parachutist is the beast (see Ch. 6, p. 107)
- mention the beast's teeth and claws, its eyes and the way it 'kind of sat up' (see Ch. 6, p. 109)
- stay with Ralph and are loyal until forced to join Jack's tribe (see Ch. 11, p. 198)
- are tortured by Roger (see Ch. 11, p. 202)
- warn Ralph about Jack and Roger's intentions to harm him (see Ch. 12, p. 211).

AIMING HIGH: DISCUSS LANGUAGE

Sam and Eric gradually become 'Samneric', just as the younger boys descend from 'little 'uns' to 'littluns'. As language is often seen as setting humankind apart from animals, this erosion of precision in the boys' language can be viewed as **symbolising** the disappearing influence of civilisation.

EXAM FOCUS: WRITING ABOUT SAM AND ERIC

Key point	Evidence/Further meaning
● The twins are so alike that nobody can tell them apart.	● 'the twins shook their heads and pointed at each other, and the crowd laughed.' (Ch. 1, p.15) ● Shows the humour created by this at the start of the novel.
● The twins are seen as a single unit.	● 'By custom now one conch did for both twins, for their substantial unity was recognized.' (Ch. 6, p. 108) ● When Sam and Eric tell of their encounter with the beast, it is as if they are telling the tale in stereo, which adds a frightening impact to the story.
● The twins are brave when confronted by Jack.	● '"You lemme go—" "—and me."' (Ch. 11, p. 202) ● Shows their resistance, initially refusing to join the savage tribe.
● The twins warn Ralph that he will be hunted and killed.	● 'They're going to hunt you tomorrow.' (Ch. 12, p. 209) ● Suggests they'd like to be on his side still. They retain civilised values but are made to do what Jack wants.

MINOR CHARACTERS

THE NAVAL OFFICER

Make sure that you focus on the relevant points when writing about the naval officer. He arrives to rescue the boys and is dismayed when he discovers they have failed to 'put up a better show' (Ch. 12, p. 224) but is that all? It is significant that he links this failure to their nationality, as Golding was concerned that many people assumed only 'enemy' nations could exhibit cruelty in war – something which he knew to be untrue. In one respect, the officer offers a sanitised view of the war. Dressed in his white, tropical kit, he could represent a rescuing knight in shining armour. However, there is irony in the boys being returned to the same war that caused the death of the parachutist – a war no less brutal than the conflict between the boys on the island.

THE PARACHUTIST

The parachutist mistaken for the beast plays a crucial role. When the boys asked for a sign from the outside world, the dead airman was not what they had in mind. They do not see him for what he is – a dead human being – but rather as a representation of defeat, death and decay.

THE LITTLUNS

Don't forget the littluns! Throughout the novel, they remain mostly anonymous. However, Golding deliberately gives the boy with the birthmark a distinguishing feature. The birthmark makes him memorable. After the overzealous fire lighting on the mountain, it is obvious that the boy is missing.

The move away from civilised behaviour towards tribalism happens early on. Notice how Percival Wemys Madison's conditioned response begins to dwindle. He fails to remember his phone number and eventually he 'sought in his head for an incantation that had faded clean away' (Ch. 12, p. 224). Golding uses minor characters to give clues about what is happening in the novel.

TOP TIP (A01)

Avoid confusing the names and roles of some minor characters. Roger is Jack's number two and Maurice is Roger's number two. Robert is one of Jack's hunters. Flick through the novel and write notes about Robert's role.

REVISION FOCUS: MAJOR AND MINOR CHARACTERS

Try making a visual representation of the characters in the novel, showing their significance in the text. You could show this through relative size, with minor characters taking up the least space, or use something like a Venn diagram or mind map to show which aspects of the plot and themes they relate to.

PROGRESS AND REVISION CHECK

SECTION ONE: CHECK YOUR KNOWLEDGE

Answer these quick questions to test your basic knowledge of the novel's characters:

1. Who are the first two characters introduced in the novel?

2. Why does Jack paint his face? (Give two reasons.)

3. Who is the littlun who at first recites his address but cannot do this at the end of the novel?

4. Why is Simon often seen as a Christ-like figure? (Give two reasons.)

5. Why do the boys elect Ralph to be leader?

6. Who has a 'compulsion to track down and kill' (Ch. 3, p. 51)?

7. What, apart from physical appearance and personality, makes Piggy different to the other boys?

8. Who does Roger throw stones around, missing him on purpose, early in the novel?

9. What is Jack's surname?

10. Who is disappointed by the boys' behaviour because they are British?

SECTION TWO: CHECK YOUR UNDERSTANDING

Here is a task about Golding's use of characters in the novel. This requires more thought and a slightly longer response. Try to write at least three to four paragraphs.

Task: Why do you think Golding included the character of Simon in *Lord of the Flies*? Think about:

- How he influences events in the novel
- His role and what he represents

PROGRESS CHECK

GOOD PROGRESS

I can:
- Explain the significance of the main characters in how the action develops. ☐
- Refer to how they are described by Golding and how this affects the way we see them. ☐

EXCELLENT PROGRESS

I can:
- Analyse in detail how Golding has shaped and developed characters over the course of the novel. ☐
- Infer key ideas, themes and issues from the ways characters and relationships are presented by Golding. ☐

THEME TRACKER A01

Good and evil

Ch. 4, p. 62: Roger's evil intentions are shown early on, when he wilfully destroys the littluns' game.

Ch. 7, pp. 125–6: Most boys, including Ralph, are caught up in the hunting game and Robert is hurt.

Ch. 10, pp. 184–6: Jack's tribe are willing to take what they want. They steal Piggy's glasses to light their fire. Their attitude has become 'might is right'.

KEY CONTEXT A03

Golding once said 'man produces evil as a bee produces honey'. Can you detect this statement in *Lord of the Flies*?

THEMES

GOOD AND EVIL

The battle between good and evil is a central theme of *Lord of the Flies* and appears in many conflicts, for example:

- Between the conch group and the savages
- Between the boys and the terrifying 'beast'
- Between attempts at rescue from a passing ship and imprisonment on the increasingly chaotic island

Early in the novel, good is in the ascendency:

- The conch provides a symbol of the decency and order of the society that the boys have come from.
- Ralph organises the construction of shelters – mostly, in fact, the selfless work of himself and Simon – and a fire to signal to ships.
- The boys spend the majority of their time playing.
- There are few accidents – although one is serious: the fire that kills the boy with the birthmark.

With Ralph's government, good is always a dominant force. When Jack forms his own tribe, evil takes control. Only the naval officer's intervention prevents its complete triumph over good.

AIMING HIGH: WRITING ABOUT EVIL

Golding experienced the Second World War and viewed it as a catalyst that released an already present evil – the original sinfulness of mankind. This trait he saw as fundamental, universal and permanent, able to emerge at any time and under any conditions.

Golding viewed children as potentially evil and sadistic. In this novel, we see stark examples of their cruelty. Jack mocks Piggy and is cruel to him from the first chapter. When Piggy suggests he can help to explore the island, Jack declares 'We don't want you' (Ch. 1, p. 21). Later on, Roger is cruel to the littluns and is willing to torture the twins.

CIVILISATION AND SAVAGERY

The shift from civilisation to savagery is a crucial theme, and the novel clearly traces a shift from one state to the other:

- Initially, the boys try to create a civilised society: the conch symbolises this through its links to democracy and order.
- The boys rapidly stop following civilised behaviour regarding eating and toileting.
- They become physically dirtier and more dishevelled.
- Violence increases gradually at first and then more rapidly.
- Jack and the hunters deliberately paint their faces like savages.
- The hunters chant and dance and make an offering to the beast.

As the boys become more savage, the consequences of their actions become more serious:

- Simon is murdered when the boys are in a frenzy and mistake him for the beast.
- Piggy is deliberately killed and Jack then gloats that 'The conch is gone!' (Ch. 11, p. 201)
- Sam and Eric are tortured and forced to join Jack's tribe.
- Ralph is hunted like an animal by the rest of the boys, who are so focused on killing him that they destroy the island.

Finally, the naval officer brings civilisation back to the island and is astonished that the boys have descended so far into savagery.

THEME TRACKER (A01)

Civilisation and savagery

Ch. 4, p. 66: Jack paints his face and feels free of the social restrictions of civilisation.

Ch. 4, p. 72: The hunting chant is first used.

Ch. 8, pp. 150–51: The sow's head is left as an offering to the beast.

KEY CONTEXT (A03)

Ideas from psychology about rational and irrational thought are placed in context by Golding. Rational thought (expressed at first by Piggy and later by Ralph) leads to civilised behaviour, such as the conch and the meetings. Irrational thought leads ultimately to savagery, such as the killing of the sow and destruction of the fruit trees.

REVISION FOCUS: DESCENT INTO SAVAGERY

Find or draw a series of pictures to represent the boys' descent into savagery. These could be pictures of scenes from the novel, or objects and symbols to represent the ideas. Assemble them into a storyboard or comic strip and use sticky notes to place a quotation with each one. Test yourself by removing the sticky notes to see if you remember them.

ORDER AND DISCIPLINE

THEME TRACKER (A01)

Order and discipline

Ch. 2, pp. 31–2: The conch is established as a token of the right to speak and Jack is excited by the idea of punishing rule breakers.

Ch. 5, pp. 84–7: Ralph calls an assembly 'to put things straight'.

Ch. 12, pp. 222–5: The naval officer represents discipline and order.

Golding was unhappy with the English public-school tradition that insisted firm discipline was the best means of turning children into young adults. He explores this idea in *Lord of the Flies*:

- There are no adults on the island. By removing them, the author sets free the impulses and desires of the schoolboys and – almost – allows them to run their full course.
- Jack first wrecks Ralph and Piggy's sensible plans, then becomes a tyrant, and finally a murderer.
- Piggy, on the other hand, is a permanent victim of Jack's bullying and is killed.

Clearly, these disasters could have been prevented by the normal orderliness of school. Is Golding despairing of the school system he taught in? Not necessarily:

- Piggy's brains and Ralph's self-discipline result in positive achievements early in the novel, such as building a fire and shelters.
- When the conch is observed, it works well as a democratic system, allowing all to be heard in an orderly manner.
- School discipline might have restricted Jack's worst excesses.
- Difficulties only arise when the arbitrary discipline of a cruel leader – Jack – emerges.

What is needed is a balance between firm discipline and a certain creative freedom, and it is the absence of this that Golding is criticising in the schools of the time.

KEY QUOTATION: JACK AND ORDER (A02)

Jack ignores agreed rules and routines many times in the novel, often explicitly challenging Ralph's leadership. One example is when he replies to Ralph's demand for Piggy's stolen specs with 'Got to? Who says?' (Ch. 11, p. 195). This demonstrates Jack's lack of concern for the order that the boys have established on the island, his short sharp questions adding a mocking tone to his refusal to accept Ralph's status as chief.

CROWD MENTALITY

THEME TRACKER (A01)

Crowd mentality

Ch. 2, pp. 37–47: The boys run off to light a fire without planning. Piggy criticises their thoughtlessness and the boy with the mulberry birthmark disappears.

Ch. 7, pp. 125–6: The first time an overexcited mob hurts a boy: Robert.

Ch. 9, pp. 167–9: Simon is murdered by a frenzied mob who think he is the beast.

Groups are important to the novel in various ways, but Golding particularly chooses to show what happens when crowd mentality is combined with a loss of order and an increase in savagery:

- The choir are already a group at the start of the novel. Their established discipline is useful in hunting.
- Pig hunts become ritualised and frenzied, marked by chants.
- Individuals are less distinct in a mob, leading them to feel absolved from blame for what the mob does. When focusing only on the hunt, the boys are unconcerned about being rescued, for example.
- The climax of this crowd mentality is Simon's murder.

The idea of crowd mentality raises the issue of individual responsibility within the novel. It is important to be aware that Golding was influenced by **existentialism** and its **philosophers**:

- They claimed that individuals were responsible for their own actions.
- If you kill someone – as the mob kill Simon – you must accept that you are responsible for your part in it, with no excuses.
- Only Ralph accepts his responsibility for Simon's death: 'That was murder' (Ch. 10, p.172). Look again at the excuses the other boys make for Simon's death.

CONFLICT: EXTERNAL AND INTERNAL

Lord of the Flies is a novel of conflicts. You may have noticed that many of the themes can be seen as opposing – or binary – pairs, for example good and evil or savagery and civilisation. It is also worth looking at the literary concept of conflict:

- There are two types of conflict in literature – external and internal.
- External conflict is when someone is up against another human, an animal, the forces of nature or anything else outside him/herself.
- Internal conflict is when a person struggles with forces within him/herself.
- How many contrasting pairs can you find in the novel?

THEME TRACKER (A01)

External conflict

Ch. 2, pp. 33–6: The boy with the birthmark first mentions a 'beastie'.

Ch. 3, pp. 50–51: Ralph struggles to build shelters against the forces of nature.

Internal conflict

Ch. 5, p. 96: Simon struggles to articulate his thoughts and is not understood.

Ch. 8, p. 156: Ralph cannot think clearly because of the shutters coming down in his mind.

EXAM FOCUS: WRITING ABOUT THE MOB (A02)

Exploring the mob could be relevant in a range of exam answers. Read this example by one student, commenting on Simon's murder:

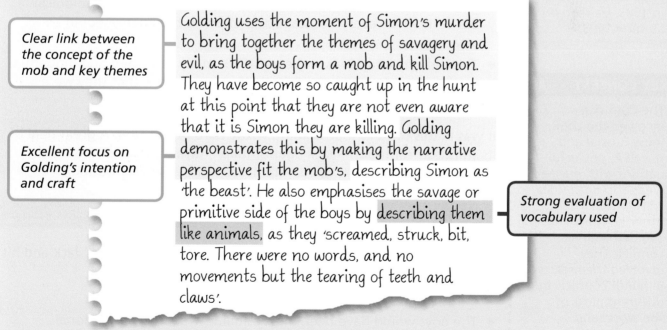

Clear link between the concept of the mob and key themes

Golding uses the moment of Simon's murder to bring together the themes of savagery and evil, as the boys form a mob and kill Simon. They have become so caught up in the hunt at this point that they are not even aware that it is Simon they are killing. Golding demonstrates this by making the narrative perspective fit the mob's, describing Simon as 'the beast'. He also emphasises the savage or primitive side of the boys by describing them like animals, as they 'screamed, struck, bit, tore. There were no words, and no movements but the tearing of teeth and claws'.

Excellent focus on Golding's intention and craft

Strong evaluation of vocabulary used

Now you try it:

This paragraph needs a final sentence or two to draw the ideas together. Add one which explains the effect of the writing here.

CONTEXTS

PERSONAL EXPERIENCES

KEY CONTEXT (A03)

William Golding, the son of a schoolmaster, was born in Cornwall on 19 September 1911. He studied Natural Sciences and then English at Brasenose College, Oxford. Later, he worked as an actor, producer and writer before teaching at Bishop Wordsworth's School, Salisbury. When the Second World War broke out, he served in the Royal Navy.

Two important elements of Golding's life and experience are powerfully reflected in *Lord of the Flies*:

- His pessimism after the Second World War
- His insight, drawn from his life as a schoolmaster, into children's behaviour

Golding sets the story in an age when the world is at war and the children are evacuated from the war zone. The novel presents his ideas that:

- Everyone is capable of evil, given the circumstances
- People were wrong, after the war, to feel relieved at not having been Nazis

He understood that being British was no protection from being evil. The British schoolchildren, as the novel closes, are prepared to kill each other.

COLD WAR PARANOIA

KEY CONTEXT (A03)

Lord of the Flies was published in 1954 and in 1961 Golding became a full-time writer. His books sold well and he received the Nobel Prize for Literature in 1983. He died on 19 June 1993.

The first use of atomic weapons in war – at Hiroshima in Japan on 6 August 1945 – undermined many people's assumptions about life:

- Suddenly it seemed possible for the whole of civilisation to be destroyed by a single conflict.
- In 1949 the Soviet Union exploded its first A-bomb and the Cold War began in earnest. This was not an open war, but was an ideological battle in which everyone suspected of being the enemy would be attacked.
- Through the late 1940s and early 1950s many respected and influential people were destroyed by (often false) accusations that they were Communists.

It was in this context that Golding wrote *Lord of the Flies*. A great deal of its stark confrontation – Jack against Ralph, savages against the conch group, even evil against good – stems from the Cold War outlook.

PUBLIC SCHOOL

KEY CONTEXT (A03)

The Cold War involved the USSR (now Russia) and the USA, powerful nations with nuclear weapons. Both sides were afraid of each other, so they avoided a direct conflict. They involved themselves in minor conflicts in different parts of the world and threatened each other, but avoided an all-out nuclear war.

It is no accident that Golding makes the school background of Jack and his choir particularly rigid in various ways:

- Choirboys would have been an elite group within a school.
- The boys would have been most familiar with an organisational structure that was hierarchical, ordered and strict.
- In the 1940s, beatings, by boys and by masters, would have been commonplace in strict schools.
- Given Jack's past conditioning, and the sudden absence of that strict regime, it is perhaps not surprising that his deeper self is released in the way we witness.

Golding's teaching experience at a public school allows him to portray Jack and his choirboys realistically:

- Jack is clearly in charge of his choir, top of the hierarchy even after the public-school structure breaks down on the island. The boys follow his strict commands, believing they cannot go against his orders.
- Roger, Jack's henchman, might well have been the school bully and appears to be allowed free rein on the island.
- Jack's desire to be chief is based on the fact that he is chapter chorister and head boy and he can 'sing C sharp' (Ch. 1, p. 18), which he feels gives him a higher status.

AIMING HIGH: COMMENT ON THE CHOIRBOYS

As well as linking the structure of the choir to the theme of order, it is also worth considering them in light of Golding's views on the nature of good and evil. Because they are associated with the Church, choirboys symbolise the ultimate in childhood innocence, allowing Golding to present the idea that evil exists in everyone.

BOYS' BEHAVIOUR

Not all the boys in the novel are from public schools. However, the boys act in some similar ways. To an extent their behaviour is reminiscent of 1940s and 1950s comic-book heroes like Roy of the Rovers, and figures of fun like Billy Bunter have clearly influenced the way in which Golding portrays the boys:

- They are initially fun-loving, with a boyish good humour.
- They also have a sense of natural decency.

All of this changes as the novel progresses.

- The boys' language remains mild, even under extreme provocation.
- Jack uses the most extreme language, towards the end of the novel.

SETTINGS

You need to be aware that the island is, in itself, a neutral place. The evil is within the boys. However, Golding uses the natural world and its creatures to foreshadow what will occur later, in various ways:

- Ralph feels that the island is good but the weather when the boys arrive is bad and the colourful bird gives a witch-like cry, which suggests that bad things will happen.
- Before Simon's death, a storm is brewing and Golding writes, 'Evening was come, not with calm beauty but with the threat of violence' (Ch. 9, p. 165). Here the island is in harmony with the boys' feelings and actions.
- As the novel ends, the island's vegetation is consumed by fire as the boys attempt to smoke out Ralph.
- Perhaps the island is the world in microcosm – a smaller version of the whole. As the adults destroy their world, so the boys are destroying the island.

TOP TIP (A02)

Golding clearly sets the novel on an island: 'We've been on the mountain-top and seen water all around. We saw no houses, no smoke, no footprints, no boats, no people.' (Ch. 2, pp. 30–1) His five repetitions of 'no' emphasise that the island is isolated. So, until the dead parachutist lands, there is nothing to distract the boys from their true natures. The island is sufficient and self-contained.

The mountain top

Castle Rock

The huts

The pool

The platform

PROGRESS AND REVISION CHECK

SECTION ONE: CHECK YOUR KNOWLEDGE

Answer these quick questions to test your basic knowledge of the themes, contexts and settings of the novel:

1. What type of person did Golding think could be truly evil?
2. What items/persons could be said to represent order in the novel?
3. What do you think is the most significant act of savagery? Why?
4. How does the island setting contribute to the novel?
5. What is the impact of the Cold War context on the novel?
6. What is the missing half of the theme '_____ and savagery'?
7. What does the 'witch-like cry' in Chapter 1 suggest about the island?
8. Which group of boys most strongly show the effect of school discipline being removed?
9. What social context of the novel best explains Jack's attitude to the other boys?
10. What drives the boys' behaviour when they hurt Robert, kill Simon and hunt Ralph?

SECTION TWO: CHECK YOUR UNDERSTANDING

Here is a task on one of Golding's themes in the novel. This requires more thought and a slightly longer response. Try to write at least three to four paragraphs.

Task: How is the idea of civilisation used in the novel? Think about:

- How the boys initially copy familiar civilised rules and patterns
- The influence of civilisation on the novel's ending

PROGRESS CHECK

GOOD PROGRESS
I can:
- Explain the main themes, contexts and settings in the text and how they contribute to the effect on the reader.
- Use a range of appropriate evidence to support any points I make about these elements.

EXCELLENT PROGRESS
I can:
- Analyse in detail the way themes are developed and presented across the novel.
- Refer closely to key aspects of context and setting and the implications they have for the writer's viewpoint, and the interpretation of relationships and ideas.

FORM

THE ADVENTURE NOVEL

TOP TIP **(A01)**

Make sure any comments you make about form are relevant to the question you are asked and the issues you are discussing. Always think about how Golding uses elements such as form to present ideas in the novel. How does knowing about *The Coral Island* help you to understand *Lord of the Flies*?

Adventure novels for children were popular in the nineteenth and early twentieth centuries. These focused on an exciting adventure, usually experienced in the outdoors by child protagonists. Examples include *Swallows and Amazons*, *Treasure Island* and *The Coral Island*.

R. M. BALLANTYNE'S *THE CORAL ISLAND* (1857)

Enormously popular, Ballantyne's novel presents three shipwrecked children – Ralph, Jack and Peterkin – enjoying an idyllic and civilised life on a Pacific island. Unlike Golding's boys, Ballantyne's encounter people (savages) on their island. They have various adventures where they save the day and act heroically.

IS *LORD OF THE FLIES* AN ADVENTURE NOVEL?

Lord of the Flies shares several key characteristics with the adventure-novel form: child characters cast away on an island; a survival plot; adventures in hunting.

However, Golding has completely reversed the morality and tone of the traditional adventure novel. In stories such as *The Coral Island*, boys encounter evil and overcome it, whereas in *Lord of the Flies*, evil within the boys gradually reveals itself and overcomes them.

KEY QUOTATIONS: *THE CORAL ISLAND* **(A03)**

Golding references *The Coral Island* by title twice in his novel. One of the boys names it in response to Ralph's 'It's like in a book' (Ch. 2, p. 33). This shows the boys' high expectations of the adventures they are going to have while awaiting rescue.

Then it is mentioned again by the naval officer at the end: 'Jolly good show. Like the Coral Island.' (Ch. 12, p. 224). Here Golding reminds us of this context in an ironic way, to highlight the enormous difference between the boys' – and naval officer's – expectations of their adventures and the tragic and terrifying reality.

REVISION FOCUS: *THE CORAL ISLAND*

Find out more about *The Coral Island* online and draw up a table of comparisons between it and *Lord of the Flies*. Can you also find out Golding's views about the relationship between the two novels?

STRUCTURE

ORGANISATION OF THE TEXT

Lord of the Flies contains twelve titled chapters. The island setting means events are largely a product of the characters' reactions and relationships as they engage with each other and their environment.

The novel's structure is dictated by the characters and setting. Apart from the naval officer and the dead parachutist, no one arrives on the island except the boys, and no one leaves – with the exception of the three who die, departing in a spiritual sense.

The boys are placed in a vacuum; the story is moved along and restructured by their social chemistry as it evolves in that restricted setting. The parachutist injects an important element, and the beast, in whatever form – dead pilot, the 'fear', or Simon mistakenly killed in its place – provides another source of tension.

The human conflicts and fear of the beast increase as the story develops. This runs alongside the gradual degeneration of morals and morale towards an inevitable climax.

> **TOP TIP** (A01)
>
> You will need to apply discussions of structure to characters, themes and ideas. For instance, time is used to show the disintegration of law and order. Place is used to show the increase in savagery. Ralph gains wisdom and, through the passage of time, is able to think things through.

CLIMAX

The climax of a novel is a dramatic point of no return. A series of events usually leads inevitably to this point, raising the stakes higher and higher.

In *Lord of the Flies,* the novel's climax is reached with Piggy's death. Various separations between Jack and Ralph lead to this point – the novel's first (and only) conscious and deliberate killing of a boy. After this point, tensions increase as Ralph is hunted, but then there is a sudden falling away at the end when Ralph, running for his life, is saved by the arrival of the naval officer.

TIME AND PLACE

The novel's structure can be analysed as distinct 'blocks' of action and development. The events take place over a period of several weeks – how many is not clear. The passage of time is suggested by one boy's loss of memory and observations about the length of the boys' hair. We also witness the disintegration of law and order and the boys' changing attitudes.

Place is important too. The first chapter is mainly set on the beach, where there is law and order, but the lighting of the fire and its burning out of control take place on the mountain. Simon's conversation with the pig's head occurs in the jungle, while the final tragedies occur at Castle Rock – Jack's domain.

LANGUAGE

OVERVIEW

William Golding's narrative style is often seen as highly descriptive and evocative, making considerable use of imagery. As he intended *Lord of the Flies* to be read as an allegory, it is not surprising that it uses many rich descriptions to create a clear mood and atmosphere. There are also many examples of irony in the novel – which, again, makes sense when you consider that he wrote to question many accepted 'truths' which he saw as incorrect and dangerous.

LANGUAGE DEVICE: DIALOGUE

What is dialogue?	Direct speech – the words characters speak to one another. Golding is careful to ensure that his characters have distinctive voices
Example	Piggy's speech is obviously working class and punctuated by grammatical errors, such as 'I didn't expect nothing' (Ch. 1, p. 8). Notice the double negative. The other boys might have said, 'I didn't expect anything.' It appears, though, that Piggy's speech and class differences are not important to the boys. What makes Piggy different is his weight and the fact that he is a hypochondriac (he worries excessively about his health).
Effect	Piggy's use of non-standard grammar is another thing that separates him from the other boys. It highlights their class differences to readers.

The language spoken by the boys is very reminiscent of the 1950s and early 1960s. Most of the boys speak middle-class standard English, the exception being Piggy.

Jack is the one boy who uses inappropriate language. He is often rude ('You shut up, you fat slug!' – Ch. 5, p. 98). His aggressive language reflects his personality. Golding has deliberately made both Piggy and Jack different, so that their characters stand out.

William Golding

TOP TIP   (A02)

Notice the boys' use of colloquial speech. Although some speech indicates class differences, all the boys use ordinary speech as if they are in an ordinary situation. For example: 'You could get someone to dress up as a pig and then he could act—you know, pretend to knock me over and all that—' (Jack, Ch. 7, p. 126). This is a key way that Golding creates realism in the novel.

LANGUAGE DEVICE: SIMILE

What is simile?	A figurative device that describes something by comparing it to something else, using 'like' or 'as'
Example	Golding describes Ralph's hair as 'full of dirt and tapped like the tendrils of a creeper' (Ch. 12, p. 203). With this simile the author creates a vivid picture of Ralph's matted, long hair.
Effect	As well as showing how filthy Ralph's hair is, this simile links his physical appearance to the jungle, making him sound wild.

As part of his descriptive style, Golding often uses vivid similes and also metaphors. These help us to appreciate the exact features that he wants to draw out – such as the thick, long and heavy feel of Ralph's hair in the example above. When writing about similes, as with all language features, you will need to explain their effect.

LANGUAGE DEVICE: IRONY

What is irony?	The use of words to express something different from, and often opposite to, their literal meaning
Example	When, at the end of novel, the naval officer says, 'Jolly good show. Like the Coral Island.' (Ch. 12, p. 224) we know that he has not understood at all. His words could not be further from the truth, highlighting how unexpected the boys' behaviour would be to the world outside.
Effect	This example underscores the difference between novels like *The Coral Island* and Golding's vision, emphasising the moral message about the boys' behaviour.

As well as direct irony in some of the things characters say, Golding also uses situational irony (where a situation is in itself ironic). For example, the survivors of the plane crash are boys evacuated from a battle zone in a world war. It is ironic that the society they form eventually breaks down and the boys are 'at war' with one another.

There is also irony present in the specific situation of some of the characters. For example, Piggy has physically weak eyesight but his insight is strong. Also, the naval officer who rescues the boys appears to be a knight in shining armour. He represents civilisation and grown-up society. However, he also represents a world at war. His world is a mirror image, on a large scale, of the island – which the boys are destroying.

Finally, there is irony in the boys' rescue being facilitated by the fire started by Jack to chase Ralph from his hiding place. Ralph is keen, throughout the novel, to keep a fire going – so that the boys have a chance of being rescued – while Jack is more interested in hunting.

KEY CONTEXT (A03)

The island itself can be seen as a metaphor for the Earth after a nuclear holocaust. Einstein once claimed that if the next world war was nuclear, the following war would be fought with bows and arrows.

LANGUAGE DEVICE: SYMBOLISM

What is symbolism?	The art of attributing symbolic meanings or significance to objects, characters, events or titles
Example	The conch, Piggy's glasses and the signal fire can all be seen as symbols of civilisation.
Effect	The symbols of civilisation in the novel operate as tokens which are controlled by different boys at different times, showing how power is used within the novel.

THE ISLAND

The island itself can be seen as a symbol, representing Paradise or the Garden of Eden before it was corrupted by humanity and original sin. Remember that Golding was a Christian and he intended to incorporate Christian ideas in his writing. Parts of the island also become symbolic: for example, the forest scar represents the corruption introduced by the boys and their plane.

PIGGY'S GLASSES

As the means of lighting a fire, the glasses relate to civilisation, because they are a tool and tool use is a sign of more advanced societies. They can also be associated with intelligence through their connection to Piggy, who is the most intelligent boy on the island. Once stolen, they are no longer used for signal fires, but only for the more basic needs of warmth and cooking, and for violence in smoking Ralph out of the forest.

THE SIGNAL FIRE

This fire represents hope, as it is key for the boys' rescue. Fire is also symbolic on the island of things getting out of control, both when the first fire is lit and at the end of the novel.

THE BEAST

The beast comes to symbolise the boys' fears. Initially a 'snake-thing', it has clear connotations of evil (linking to the Garden of Eden, like the island itself). Eventually, the beast is revealed to actually be a dead parachutist – a symbol of the destruction going on in the outside world.

CHARACTERS AS SYMBOLS

Golding also clearly makes his characters symbolise key ideas in the text. Piggy represents logic and clear rationality, Ralph is the symbol of order and civilisation, while Jack represents savagery. In a reading of the text as a political allegory, Ralph (along with the conch) represents democracy, while Jack stands for totalitarianism. In a Freudian psychological reading, Jack symbolises the id, Piggy the superego and Ralph the ego.

PROGRESS AND REVISION CHECK

SECTION ONE: CHECK YOUR KNOWLEDGE

Answer these quick questions to test your basic knowledge of the form, structure and language of the novel:

1. State two links between *The Coral Island* and *Lord of the Flies*.

2. Explain one way in which the novel is allegorical.

3. What does the conch symbolise?

4. Why is Piggy's language different from the other boys'?

5. How is the language device of irony used in the novel?

6. How does Golding show the passage of time on the island?

7. What is the novel's climax?

8. Name three language devices which Golding uses frequently.

9. What symbolises the boys' damaging effect on the island?

10. What is ironic about the fire in the final chapter?

SECTION TWO: CHECK YOUR UNDERSTANDING

Here is a task on Golding's use of language in the novel. This requires more thought and a slightly longer response. Try to write at least three to four paragraphs.

Task: How important is description and imagery in *Lord of the Flies*? Think about:

● What Golding uses description and imagery for
● Significant examples of description and/or imagery

PROGRESS CHECK

GOOD PROGRESS

I can:

● Explain how the writer uses form, structure and language to develop the action, show relationships, and develop ideas. ☐

● Use relevant quotations to support the points I make, and refer to the effect of some language choices. ☐

EXCELLENT PROGRESS

I can:

● Analyse in detail Golding's use of particular forms, structures and language techniques to convey ideas, create characters, and evoke mood or setting. ☐

● Select from a range of evidence, including apt quotations, to infer the effect of particular language choices, and to develop wider interpretations. ☐

UNDERSTANDING THE QUESTION

For your exam, you will be answering a question on the whole text and/or a question on an extract from *Lord of the Flies*. Check with your teacher to see what sort of question you are doing. Whatever the task, questions in exams will need **decoding**. This means highlighting and understanding the key words so that the answer you write is relevant.

BREAK DOWN THE QUESTION

TOP TIP (A01)

You might also be asked to 'refer closely to', which means picking out specific examples from the text, or to focus on 'methods and techniques', which means the 'things' Golding does, for example, the use of a particular language feature, an ironic comment on an event, etc.

Pick out the **key words** or phrases. For example:

Question: How does William Golding **present ideas** about **leadership** in *Lord of the Flies*. Write about:

● Ideas about leadership in *Lord of the Flies*
● How Golding presents these ideas by the way he writes

What does this tell you?

● Focus on the theme **of leadership** but also on **'ideas'** – for example, different characters' views on leadership.
● The word **'present'** tells you that you should focus on how Golding reveals these ideas, i.e. the techniques he uses.

PLANNING YOUR ANSWER

It is vital that you generate ideas quickly, and plan your answer efficiently when you sit the exam. Stick to your plan, and with a watch at your side, tick off each part as you progress.

STAGE 1: GENERATE IDEAS QUICKLY

Very briefly **list your key ideas** based on the question you have **decoded**. For example:

● *Ralph's use of the conch – democracy*
● *Ralph's planning and thought before key meetings*
● *Jack's promises of meat and fun*
● *Jack's use of violence*

STAGE 2: JOT DOWN USEFUL QUOTATIONS (OR KEY EVENTS)

For example:

● 'I ought to be chief ... because I'm chapter chorister and head boy. I can sing C sharp.' (Ch. 1, p. 18)

● 'the conch doesn't count up here' (Ch. 9, p. 166)

STAGE 3: PLAN FOR PARAGRAPHS

Use paragraphs to plan your answer. For example:

Paragraph	Point
Paragraph 1:	**Introduce** the **argument** you wish to make: *Golding presents two contrasting approaches to leadership: democratic and totalitarian. He uses Jack and Ralph to represent these approaches, which are also linked to the theme of civilisation and savagery.*
Paragraph 2:	Your first point: *Ralph represents democracy: he uses the conch to allow others to express their views in meetings.* Expand and add further example.
Paragraph 3:	Your second point: *Jack stands for totalitarianism. He believes he personally deserves power.* Expand and add further example.
Paragraph 4:	Your third point: *Ralph's democratic leadership is based on good sense and practicality. He represents civilisation and thinks about long-term issues such as planning for rescue.* Give examples such as *When ....*
Paragraph 5:	Your fourth point: *Jack's totalitarian leadership is based on personal power and represents savagery. He promises fun and meat and later uses threats and violence to control the others.* Give examples such as *When ....*
[You may want to add further paragraphs if you have time.]	
Conclusion:	**Sum up** your argument: *Leadership is a key idea in the novel, linked to other key themes and played out through the characters. The novel as a whole shows the consequences of accepting totalitarian or savage leadership.*

TOP TIP (A02)

When discussing Golding's language, make sure you refer to the techniques he uses and, most important, the **effect** of those techniques. Don't just say, *Golding uses lots of description here.* Write: *Golding's use of description shows [or demonstrates or conveys] the ideas that ....*

RESPONDING TO WRITERS' EFFECTS

The two most important assessment objectives are **AO1** and **AO2**. They are about *what* writers do (the choices they make, and the effects these create), *what* your ideas are (your analysis and interpretation), and *how* you write about them (how well you explain your ideas).

ASSESSMENT OBJECTIVE 1

What does it say?	What does it mean?	Dos and Don'ts
Read, understand and respond to texts. Students should be able to: ● Maintain a critical style and develop an informed personal response ● Use textual references, including quotations, to support and illustrate interpretations	You must: ● Use some of the literary terms you have learned (correctly!) ● Write in a professional way (not a sloppy, chatty way) ● Show you have thought for yourself ● Back up your ideas with examples, including quotations	**Don't write:** *Ralph is a good character. Golding describes him using nice words like 'fair'. He has 'a mildness about his mouth and eyes that proclaimed no devil.'* **Do write:** *Golding consistently presents Ralph as a moral and decent character. For example, in Chapter 1, when Golding describes him as having 'a mildness' to his face which 'proclaimed no devil', using the noun 'mildness' shows that he is gentle.*

IMPROVING YOUR CRITICAL STYLE

Use a variety of words and phrases to show effects:

Golding *suggests ..., conveys ..., implies ..., explores ..., demonstrates ..., signals ..., describes how ..., shows how ..... I/we* (as readers) *infer ..., recognise ..., understand ..., question...*

For example, look at these two paragraphs by different students about Piggy. Note the difference in the quality of expression.

Student A:

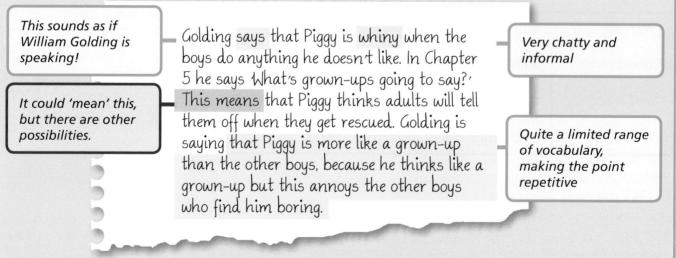

This sounds as if William Golding is speaking!

It could 'mean' this, but there are other possibilities.

Golding says that Piggy is whiny when the boys do anything he doesn't like. In Chapter 5 he says 'What's grown-ups going to say?' This means that Piggy thinks adults will tell them off when they get rescued. Golding is saying that Piggy is more like a grown-up than the other boys, because he thinks like a grown-up but this annoys the other boys who find him boring.

Very chatty and informal

Quite a limited range of vocabulary, making the point repetitive

Student B:

Good level of vocabulary

Neat way to also show a wider appreciation of Piggy's character

Golding presents Piggy as the boys' link to the adult world when he criticises their behaviour. For example, in Chapter 5 he asks, 'What's grown-ups going to say?' This reveals his expectation that they will be rescued and have to explain themselves to adults. This is one of many times that Golding explicitly links Piggy with grown-up thought, perhaps to remind us that he represents reason and an adult outlook.

This helps the student include another idea about Piggy by examining assumptions behind his speech

Explores the idea rather than stating it bluntly as fact

ASSESSMENT OBJECTIVE 2

What does it say?	What does it mean?	Dos and Don'ts
Analyse the language, form and structure used by the writer to create meanings and effects, using relevant subject terminology where appropriate.	'Analyse' – comment **in detail** on **particular aspects** of the text or language. 'Language' – vocabulary, imagery, variety of sentences, dialogue/speech, etc. 'Form' – how the story is told (e.g. first person narrative, letters, diaries, chapter by chapter?) 'Structure' – the order in which events are revealed, or in which characters appear, or descriptions are presented 'Create meaning' – what can we, as readers, infer from what the writer tells us? What is implied by particular descriptions, or events? 'Subject terminology' – words you should use when writing about novels, such as protagonist, **imagery**, **setting**, etc.	**Don't write:** *The writing is really descriptive in this bit so I get a good picture of the island.* **Do write:** *Golding **conveys** the sense that the island **setting** is significant, as it is **presented** with **connotations** of both tranquillity and danger. Golding's use of the awkward-sounding phrase 'interrupted abruptly' (makes the platform sound like an intrusion on the landscape, while the **nouns** 'coolness and shade' imply that it is a safe place.*

THE THREE 'I'S

● The best analysis focuses on specific ideas, events or uses of language and thinks about what is **implied.**

● This means looking beyond the obvious and beginning to draw **inferences.** On the surface, Golding's initial description of the island is visual, but what deeper ideas are suggested about how the setting will affect the boys' adventure?

● From the inferences you make across the text as a whole, you can arrive at your own **interpretation** – a sense of the bigger picture, a wider evaluation of a person, relationship or idea.

USING QUOTATIONS

One of the secrets of success in writing exam essays is to use quotations **effectively**. There are five basic principles:

1. Quote only what is most useful.
2. Do not use a quotation that repeats what you have just written.
3. Put quotation marks, e.g. ' ', around the quotation.
4. Write the quotation exactly as it appears in the original.
5. Use the quotation so that it fits neatly into your sentence.

EXAM FOCUS: USING QUOTATIONS (A01)

Quotations should be used to develop the line of thought in your essay and 'zoom in' on key details, such as language choices. The example below shows a clear and effective way of doing this:

> **Quotation** — Golding presents Simon as different to the other boys. He describes him as having 'eyes so bright' that Ralph thought he would be good fun. This suggests that Simon is more serious than Ralph at first believed him to be.
>
> **Point**
> **Explanation/effect**

However, really **high-level responses** will go further. They will make an even more precise point, support it with an even more appropriate quotation, focus on particular words and phrases and explain the effect or what is implied to make a wider point or draw inferences. Here is an example:

> **Quotation (more precise)**
> **Explanation/implication/effect** — Golding presents Simon as a surprisingly serious young boy whose 'eyes' were 'so bright they had deceived Ralph'. The use of the verb 'deceived' implies that Simon's appearance is deliberately different to his personality, emphasising that he is not what he at first appears. This encourages us as readers to pay closer attention to what Simon says and does to have a better understanding of him.
>
> **Precise point**
> **Language feature**
> **Further development/link**

SPELLING, PUNCTUATION AND GRAMMAR

SPELLING

Remember to spell correctly the **author's** name, the names of all the **characters**, and the **names of places**.

A good idea is to list some of the key spellings you know you sometimes get wrong **before** the exam starts. Then use your list to check as you go along. Sometimes it is easy to make small errors as you write but if you have your key word list nearby you can check spellings.

PUNCTUATION

Remember:

- Use **full stops and commas in sentences accurately to make clear** points. Don't write long, rambling sentences that don't make sense. Equally, avoid using a lot of short repetitive sentences. Write in a fluent way, using linking words and phrases, and use **inverted commas** for **quotations**.

Don't write	Do write
Ralph and Jack are opposites they move further apart from each other as the novel progresses this may be because they show different kinds of leadership.	*Ralph and Jack are opposites who move further apart from each other as the novel progresses. This may be because they show different kinds of leadership.*

GRAMMAR

When you are writing about the text, make sure you:

- Use the present tense for discussing what the writer does, e.g. *Golding **presents** Ralph as a practical and realistic leader* not *Golding **presented** Ralph as a practical and realistic leader.*
- Use pronouns and references back to make your writing flow.

Don't write	Do write
Although Piggy represents logic in the novel, Piggy's use of less standard language and stronger accent than the other boys showed that Piggy was less well educated than the other boys.	*Although Piggy represents logic in the novel, **his** use of less standard language and stronger accent than the other boys **shows** that **he is** less well educated than **them**.*

TOP TIP (A04)

Remember that spelling, punctuation and grammar are worth **approximately 5%** of your overall marks, which could mean the difference between one grade and another.

TOP TIP (A04)

Practise your spellings of key literature terms you might use when writing about the text such as: ironic, omnipotent narrator, simile, metaphor, allegory, symbolism, imagery, protagonist, character, theme, **hierarchy**, etc.

TOP TIP (A04)

Enliven your essay by varying the way your sentences begin. For example, *Ralph and Piggy have to approach Jack's tribe, although they are scared of them* can also be written as: *Although they are scared of them, Ralph and Piggy have to approach Jack's tribe.*

ANNOTATED SAMPLE ANSWERS

This section provides three sample responses, one at **mid** level, one at a **good** level and one at a **very high** level.

Question: How does Golding present ideas about power in the novel?

Write about:

- How Golding uses particular characters to explore power
- How Golding presents these ideas by the way he writes

SAMPLE ANSWER 1

A01 Introduces key idea about power

Golding presents ideas about power through the boys' leadership struggles in the novel. He uses the novel to show that power can be abused and that some people just want power for themselves.

A01 Specific point of view

A04 Topic sentence to open new paragraph

He uses Ralph to show a fair and sensible way of having power. Ralph is a practical character who shares power with the other boys, in which he uses the conch as a symbol to show who is allowed to talk. He says that this is 'like at school', referring to familiar rules from home and linking to the theme of civilisation. He is clearly thinking about fairness and practicality, if everyone talks at once then meetings will not work properly.

A04 Inaccurate use of punctuation (comma splice)

A02 Quotation supports point and is explained although it could be explored in more detail

The way that Ralph gains power is also fair because all the boys vote for him to be chief except for the choirboys because they are probably frightened of Jack as he is a bully. A lot of the younger boys only vote for Ralph because he has the conch, as though having the conch has made them respect him without him doing anything. He does turn out to have good leadership skills, though, like when he goes away to think and plan for the meeting: 'Ralph was a specialist in thought now, and could recognise thought in another.'

A01 Quite an informal style

A02 Clear reference quotation but needs closer analysis and further explanation

With Ralph, Golding is showing what he wants us to see as the right way of having power. Ralph gets power fairly, thinks carefully about what is right and also plans for the longer term, like building shelters even though it's hard work and many of the boys would rather be hunting or playing.

He is also the one who insists on having the fire for a signal, as he keeps hoping for rescue.

A01 This paragraph makes reasonable points but lacks specific examples or analytical detail

Unlike Ralph, Jack thinks about power because he definitely wants to have it and takes it by bribery and force. Where Ralph represents democracy and fairness, Jack's leadership is intended to be like totalitarian powers such as Nazi Germany or Russia, showing that Golding wanted his readers to see how power could be violent and corrupt.

A03 Clear and appropriate reference to Golding's context

Jack believes that he should have power because of his skills, which are about being a good choirboy so they are not likely to be much use on the island, 'I ought to be chief ... I can sing C sharp'. He thinks he has a right to power because of who he is, but he doesn't think at all about what being a good leader would mean on the island.

A01 Well selected quotation

Once things start going wrong on the island, Jack tries to take power away from Ralph by encouraging the boys to hunt with him. He bribes them by saying they can have fun as the boys enjoy hunting with chanting and drumming, and then later when Jack has won over most of the boys with these bribes, he switches to violence as a means of control. Jack shows the dangers of power.

A01 Clear conclusion tying key ideas together

In the novel, Golding presents ideas about power mostly through the characters of Ralph and Jack, who represent different approaches to power.

MID LEVEL

Comment
There are some good points made here and a viewpoint comes across but the style is rather chatty and informal in places. The writer needs to refer more to Golding himself and what **he** does, and there is little reference to language devices or techniques. There is one comment on context but it is quite broad. Ideas are generally made clear, but language is not always used precisely.

For a Good Level:
- Use a more formal and critical vocabulary rather than chatty, informal words and phrases.
- Embed quotations into sentences so that they flow and are easy to follow.
- Comment in detail on the effect of language choices made by Golding.

SAMPLE ANSWER 2

A01 Key idea for essay is introduced immediately

The key way that Golding explores ideas about power is by using his characters. 'Lord of the Flies' is an allegorical novel, with characters symbolising different approaches to power. Golding uses Jack to represent a totalitarian approach, and Ralph to represent democracy. The other boys are used to show how easily totalitarian power can become successful. Ultimately, Jack's power is only halted by the arrival of the naval officer, representing the outside adult world.

Golding shows that, at first, power is organised democratically. Ralph finds the conch and, with Piggy's help, uses it to call the other boys, who see him as a natural leader because of his possession of this powerful object. Golding shows us how important the conch is through Piggy's attitude to it: Piggy ... stroked the glistening thing that lay in Ralph's hands.' Using the verb 'stroked' shows Piggy's delicate and respectful treatment of the conch.

A01 Useful focus on the writer

A02 Zooms in on key word and explains its effect

Golding shows Jack's assumption that he 'ought to be chief' because he 'can sing C sharp' during the first discussion about power on the island. Clearly in the boys' new situation, this is an irrelevant skill, so Golding is making it clear that Jack believes he deserves power simply because he is used to having it. In the vote, the choristers are the only ones who do not vote for Ralph, perhaps providing a hint of Jack's power to come.

A01 Quotation effectively embedded into sentence

A01 Evidence of overview of text, linking to later events

A03 Clear link to context in relevant way

Golding shows his ideas about human nature through the novel and one of the ideas he wanted to explore was the idea that some people are evil and others good. Having served in the Second World War, he had seen that anyone is capable of evil – it was blatantly not the case that all Nazis were bad and Allies were good, so he wanted to show that ordinary people, even innocent-seeming schoolboys, could be overtaken by evil and let it have power. The way power shifts from the civilised rule of order to the savage and primitive tribe led by Jack shows this.

A01 Rather informal phrasing

A04 Repetitive paragraph opening

Golding shows the way that the power balance changes on the

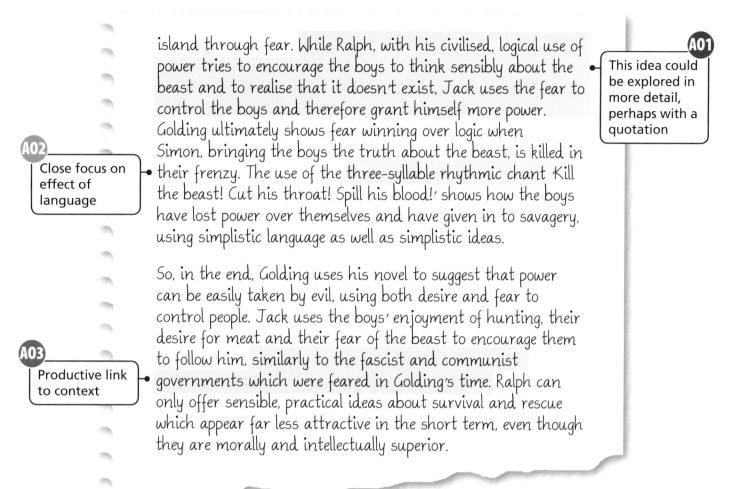

A01
This idea could be explored in more detail, perhaps with a quotation

A02
Close focus on effect of language

A03
Productive link to context

island through fear. While Ralph, with his civilised, logical use of power tries to encourage the boys to think sensibly about the beast and to realise that it doesn't exist, Jack uses the fear to control the boys and therefore grant himself more power. Golding ultimately shows fear winning over logic when Simon, bringing the boys the truth about the beast, is killed in their frenzy. The use of the three-syllable rhythmic chant 'Kill the beast! Cut his throat! Spill his blood!' shows how the boys have lost power over themselves and have given in to savagery, using simplistic language as well as simplistic ideas.

So, in the end, Golding uses his novel to suggest that power can be easily taken by evil, using both desire and fear to control people. Jack uses the boys' enjoyment of hunting, their desire for meat and their fear of the beast to encourage them to follow him, similarly to the fascist and communist governments which were feared in Golding's time. Ralph can only offer sensible, practical ideas about survival and rescue which appear far less attractive in the short term, even though they are morally and intellectually superior.

GOOD LEVEL

Comment
This is a generally fluent and well-argued response which explores the idea of power in the novel in some detail. There is some close analysis of key words and phrases to get points across, and relevant usage of contextual information. Expression is generally good, and quotations are fluently embedded, but use of words such as 'blatantly' may be a little too informal.

For a High Level:
● Analyse Golding's use of language, form and structure more frequently.
● Expand the style of expression by using a wider vocabulary so more subtle ideas can be developed.
● Vary opening sentences in paragraphs so that the essay can introduce ideas in more interesting ways.

SAMPLE ANSWER 3

A01 Excellent opening introduction sets up centrality of the idea of power

Power is crucial to 'Lord of the Flies'. Golding takes his representatives of humanity and places them on an uninhabited island in order to demonstrate how the desire for power corrupts and leads to tragedy. He uses innocent schoolboys – choirboys, no less – to people his allegory in order that the naturalness of evil can be made absolutely clear. There can be no question that the boys cause their own disaster, and the struggle for power is absolutely at the centre of it.

A02 Clear overview introducing the idea of allegory

A02 Clear summary of three allegorical interpretations, all linked to the question

A complex and well-constructed allegory, the novel has more than one apparently intended interpretation. It can be seen as a biblical allegory relating to the Fall, a political allegory showing the dangers of totalitarianism, and a psychological allegory presenting the struggle between the id, the ego and the superego. In each of these allegories, the balance of power is at the heart of the struggle.

Golding reveals the biblical allegory through the character of Simon and the symbol of the Lord of the Flies. Simon's role is to attempt to show the boys the truth about the beast but, like Christ, to be ignored and eventually killed as the mob demands blood. Golding presents the moment of Simon's murder as inhuman: 'There were no words, and no movements but the tearing of teeth and claws.' The power in this moment belongs to the mob, who ironically are incapable of wielding any power but physical violence. Golding's repetition of the negative 'no' here, coupled first with the noun 'words', emphasises the uncivilised (or pre-civilised) nature of the boys at this point as language is taken to be a key differentiator between man and beast. The nouns associated with the mob instead, 'teeth' and 'claws', underscore this point and firmly paint the boys as savage and inhuman.

A01 Focus on the question retained

A02 Excellent development analysing language in depth

A04 Paragraphs and ideas clearly linked together in a coherent structure

The political allegory is clearly the most explicitly linked to power, however, depicting the struggle between Ralph and democracy on one hand and Jack and totalitarianism on the other. As the boys gradually move away from order and good sense, they become more primitive and respect Jack's version of leadership more. Golding's novel reflects

A01 Conceptual approach showing clear overview of novel consistently offered

contemporary fears about regimes such as communist Russia, while he clearly demonstrates his view that such things could happen to anyone, anywhere – no-one, not even British choristers, is safe from the lure of totalitarian power.

A03 Concise and focused reference to context

Golding uses the character of Jack to represent the desire for power for its own sake. Jack's arrogance is shown immediately with his claim 'I ought to be chief' implying a moral and automatic right to power with the modal verb 'ought', juxtaposed with his absurd reasoning: he should have power because he had power before and he 'can sing C sharp' – clearly a skill with no relevance in his new island setting. However, at the same time, Ralph's selection as chief is no more sensible, since the boys choose him seemingly purely on the grounds that he has the conch: 'Let him be chief with the trumpet-thing.' The conch itself has such power that merely being in possession of it is enough to bestow Ralph with leadership qualities. Although Golding presents Ralph as a good leader later, he does not seem to be recommending democratic leaders as inherently valuable either.

A02 Detailed and concise analysis of language

In terms of Freudian interpretations, the novel demonstrates what happens when the id (Jack) is able to run rampant and figuratively destroy the superego (Piggy), despite the ego's (Ralph's) best efforts. This interpretation is perhaps the best explanation for Piggy's unsympathetic presentation early in the book: the superego may often be right, but the voice of reason is usually unpopular. Golding demonstrates the powerful urge to let the id rule, but also shows how dangerous an impulse this is.

A04 Concise presentation of ideas

In conclusion, power is a concept running throughout the novel and affecting every possible interpretation. Ultimately, Golding brings adult power back in the form of the naval officer, as the boys' society has broken down beyond any chance of repair. Interestingly, even Jack reverts instantly to the status of 'a little boy' in the presence of the officer, as Golding uses external intervention to rescue the boys. In the end, however, they are only physically saved, as morally they can be seen as beyond redemption, having suffered 'the loss of innocence' in the power struggle between rival factions on the island

A01 Conclusion draws ideas together and offers an interpretation of the novel's ending

VERY HIGH LEVEL

Comment
This articulate response explores a range of ideas, giving a thorough analysis of the novel's allegorical meanings combined with very close language analysis.

PRACTICE TASK

Write a full-length response to this exam-style question and then use the **Mark scheme** on page 80 to assess your response.

> How does Golding explore the connected ideas of savagery and civilisation in *Lord of the Flies*?
>
> Write about:
>
> - The ideas about savagery and civilisation in *Lord of the Flies*
> - How Golding presents these ideas by the ways he writes

TOP TIP

You can use the General skills section of the **Mark scheme** on page 80 to remind you of the key criteria you'll need to cover.

Remember:

- Plan quickly and efficiently by using key words from the question
- Focus on the techniques Golding uses and the effect of these on the reader
- Support your ideas with relevant evidence, including quotations

FURTHER QUESTIONS

 How does Golding use the character of Jack to explore ideas about evil?

Write about:

- How Golding presents the character of Jack
- How Golding uses Jack to present ideas about evil

2 'What I mean is … maybe it's only us.' How is the concept of the beast important in *Lord of the Flies*? You **must** refer to the context of the novel in your answer.

3 Answer both parts of this question:

(a) Read from 'After they had eaten …' to '… the chief would have to go forward' (Ch. 6, pp. 112–13). Look at how Simon speaks and behaves here. What does it reveal about his character at this point in the novel? Refer closely to details from the extract to support your answer.

(b) *Lord of the Flies* is about 'things breaking down'. To what extent do you agree with this view of the novel? Give reasons for what you say.

LITERARY TERMS

allegory	a story with two different meanings, where the straightforward meaning on the surface is used to reveal a deeper meaning underneath
antagonist	a leading character in a novel, play or film who opposes the main protagonist
atmosphere	a mood or feeling
character	either a person in a play, novel, etc., or his or her personality
climax	the turning point at which the conflict begins to resolve itself or the final and most exciting event
colloquial	the everyday speech used by people in ordinary situations
connotations	associations brought to mind by a word or phrase, for example 'scrawny' has negative connotations of being unhealthy and unattractive while 'skinny' may have more positive connotations
dramatic irony	when the reader (audience) knows more about what is happening than some of the characters
flashback	a sudden jumping back to an earlier point in the narrative
foreshadow	act as a warning or sign of something that will occur later
imagery	descriptive language which uses images to make actions, objects and characters more vivid in the reader's mind. Metaphors and similes are examples of imagery.
irony/ironic	when somebody deliberately says one thing when they mean another, usually in a humorous or sarcastic way
metaphor	when one thing is used to describe another thing to create a striking or unusual image
narrative perspective	the point of view or perspective from which a story or any recital of events is told: for example, first-person narratives (using 'I') are told from a character's perspective. More than one narrative perspective may be used within a text.
omniscient narrator	a narrator who uses the third person ('he', 'she', 'they') and who has access to all the thoughts and feelings of the characters and to the events that take place
onomatopoeia	the use of words which sound like the noise they describe
pathetic fallacy	when the natural world, especially the weather, is used to reflect the feelings of characters
protagonist	a leading character in a novel, play or film
simile	when one thing is compared directly to another thing, using the word 'like' or 'as'
structure	the organisation or overall design of a work
symbol/symbolism	when an object, a person or a thing is used to represent another thing
theme	a central idea examined by an author

CHECKPOINT ANSWERS

CHECKPOINT 1, page 11

Two: Jack Merridew and Percy Wemys Madison.

CHECKPOINT 2, page 12

'the snake thing' (Ch. 2, p. 34)

CHECKPOINT 3, page 14

Read Chapter 3, pp. 51–2 carefully to check that your evidence is correct and complete.

CHECKPOINT 4, page 15

They are playing on the beach and swimming.

CHECKPOINT 5, page 16

Maurice.

CHECKPOINT 6, page 17

He enjoys the thrill of hunting.

CHECKPOINT 7, page 18

Their general dirtiness and lack of hygiene.

CHECKPOINT 8, page 19

He has been bullied in the past.

CHECKPOINT 9, page 20

His arrival on the island proves there is life outside. War has not annihilated (totally destroyed) civilisation.

CHECKPOINT 10, page 22

It enables him to understand the actions of others and how to have sympathy with them.

CHECKPOINT 11, page 22

They are arguing about courage ... or lack of it!

CHECKPOINT 12, page 24

He is relieved to see Jack gone.

CHECKPOINT 13, page 25

The voice of authority – the voice of one who is always right.

CHECKPOINT 14, page 25

He is concerned about the other boys, particularly the safety of the younger children.

CHECKPOINT 15, page 26

There are various possible answers to this question but your opinion should be based on evidence from the novel or its context.

CHECKPOINT 16, page 27

They are both washed out to sea.

CHECKPOINT 17, page 29

He refers to it as an accident.

CHECKPOINT 18, page 29

He avoids discussions and issues orders.

CHECKPOINT 19, page 31

The conch.

CHECKPOINT 20, page 33

The savagery of the island.

PROGRESS AND REVISION CHECK ANSWERS

PART TWO, pages 35–6

SECTION ONE

1. Their evacuation plane crashed
2. The choir
3. On the mountain
4. Simon
5. Clay
6. Think
7. Simon
8. Piggy
9. Robert
10. Ralph
11. The sow's head
12. The Lord of the Flies
13. A (thunder)storm
14. That the parachutist is 'the beast'
15. An accident
16. Eric
17. Piggy's glasses
18. The conch
19. Samneric
20. Because the boys are crying

SECTION TWO

Task 1:

- Jack seems to become someone else: 'an awesome stranger' (Ch. 4, p. 66).
- He feels free of society's rules: 'liberated from shame and self-consciousness' (Ch. 4, p. 66).
- We see that he wants to escape from civilisation, as he celebrates the freedom: 'He capered' (Ch. 4, p. 66).
- The other boys fear the mask but are also attracted to the idea: 'a mask that drew their eyes and appalled them' (Ch. 4, p. 66).

Task 2:

- Simon feels like an outsider but wants to be included: 'You don't want Ralph to think you're batty do you?' (Ch. 8, p. 157)
- We see that Simon could be in danger: 'we shall do you'. (Ch. 8, p. 159)
- Many questions asked by the pig's head make it in control of the conversation: 'Aren't you just a silly little boy?' (Ch. 8, p. 157)
- Unusual verb emphasises danger: 'the laughter shivered' (Ch. 8, p. 158)

PART THREE, page 47

SECTION ONE

1. Ralph and Piggy

2. So the pigs won't see him, to feel more like a hunter and to feel free of civilisation

3. Percival Wemys Madison

4. He makes predictions, he sees what others don't and he is martyred

5. Because he has the conch

6. Jack

7. He is working class and/or his accent

8. Henry

9. Merridew

10. The naval officer

SECTION TWO

- Simon talking to the pig's head shows how the beast is within the boys: 'we shall do you. See? Jack and Roger and Maurice and Robert and Bill and Piggy and Ralph.' (Ch. 8, p. 159)

- Simon tries to show the boys the truth about the beast, but they are too frenzied to listen and kill him: 'the crowd surged after it … screamed, struck, bit, tore.' (Ch. 9, p. 169)

- Simon is mysterious and not like the others. He predicts future events: 'You'll get back to where you came from.' (Ch. 7, p. 121)

- Simon represents good and truth. He can be seen as Christ figure, trying to teach the boys but not being heard: 'You're batty.' (Ch. 7, p. 121)

PART FOUR, page 55

SECTION ONE

1. Anyone

2. The conch, the glasses, Ralph, Piggy

3. Answers will vary but could include: making the offering of the pig's head, killing Simon, killing Piggy, hunting Ralph.

4. It seems like paradise but is infected by the boys and/or it isolates the boys so they are not subject to outside influences.

5. Answers will vary but could include: the boys' crashing onto the island, the representation of communist totalitarianism in Jack.

6. Civilisation

7. That there is danger or that it is not solely a paradise

8. The choirboys or hunters

9. Public school, where the head choirboy would have been a figure of authority

10. Crowd/mob mentality

SECTION TWO

- The boys' meetings are initially civilised: 'We can't have everybody talking at once.' (Ch. 2, p. 31)

- The boys have rules about hygiene to begin with: 'We chose those rocks right along beyond the bathing-pool as a lavatory.' (Ch. 5, p. 85)

- It is ironic that the fire lit to smoke Ralph out leads to their rescue: 'We saw your smoke.' (Ch. 12, p. 224)

- The naval officer assumes that the boys have brought civilisation to the island: 'Like the Coral Island.' (Ch. 12, p. 224)

PART FIVE, page 61

SECTION ONE

1 Boys named Ralph and Jack (and Peterkin) are stranded on an island, they hunt and gather food and build shelters.

2 The island represents Paradise and the boys bring sin onto it (the Fall) or Ralph's leadership represents democracy while Jack's represents totalitarianism (communism/fascism) or the three main characters represent parts of the psyche: Jack is the id, Piggy the superego and Ralph the ego.

3 Democracy, order and/or civilisation

4 To show he is of a lower social class

5 Characters make statements which are the opposite of what is true.

6 The length of the boys' hair increases.

7 Piggy's death

8 Any three of the following: simile, irony, metaphor, dialogue, symbolism

9 The scar where the plane crashed

10 Jack does not care about fires for signalling, but this fire, lit to catch Ralph, acts as the signal which results in the boys' rescue.

SECTION TWO

- The initial description of the island shows its possibilities as peaceful but also potentially dangerous: 'a bird, a vision of red and yellow, flashed upward with a witch-like cry' (Ch. 1, p. 1)

- The fire that gets out of control in Chapter 2 is presented like a living thing to emphasise how it seems to have a mind of its own: 'scrambled up like a bright squirrel' (Ch. 2, p. 44)

- The storm preceding Simon's death creates a violent and threatening atmosphere: 'the blue-white scar jagged above them and the sulphurous explosion beat down.' (Ch. 9, p. 168)

- The final description of Jack takes away all his power: 'A little boy who wore the remains of an extraordinary black cap on his red hair and who carried the remains of a pair of spectacles at his waist' (Ch. 12, p. 224).

MARK SCHEME

POINTS YOU COULD HAVE MADE

Golding explores the connected ideas of savagery and civilisation in various ways:

- Conch as symbol of civilisation
- Jack's and Ralph's different ideas about the purpose of rules
- Ralph and Piggy's focus on order: huts, hygiene, signal fire

- Jack's links to savagery
- Mask as symbol of savagery
- Lord of the Flies as evidence of savage beliefs/ practices
- Chanting as savagery
- Death of Piggy linked to destruction of conch

GENERAL SKILLS

Make a judgement about your level based on the points you made (above) and the skills you showed.

Level	Key elements	Spelling, punctuation and grammar	Tick your level
Very high	**Very well-structured answer which gives a rounded and convincing viewpoint.** You use very detailed analysis of the writer's methods and effects on the reader, using precise references which are fluently woven into what you say. You draw inferences, consider more than one perspective or angle, including the context where relevant, and make interpretations about the text as a whole.	You spell and punctuate with consistent accuracy, and use a very wide range of vocabulary and sentence structures to achieve effective control of meaning.	
Good to high	**A thoughtful, detailed response with well-chosen references.** At the top end, you address all aspects of the task in a clearly expressed way, and examine key aspects in detail. You are beginning to consider implications, explore alternative interpretations or ideas; at the top end, you do this fairly regularly and with some confidence.	You spell and punctuate with considerable accuracy, and use a considerable range of vocabulary and sentence structures to achieve general control of meaning.	
Mid	**A consistent response with clear understanding of the main ideas shown.** You use a range of references to support your ideas and your viewpoint is logical and easy to follow. Some evidence of commenting on writers' effects, though more needed.	You spell and punctuate with reasonable accuracy, and use a reasonable range of vocabulary and sentence structures.	
Lower	**Some relevant ideas but an inconsistent and rather simple response in places.** You show you have understood the task and you make some points to support what you say, but the evidence is not always well chosen. Your analysis is a bit basic and you do not comment in much detail on the writer's methods.	Your spelling and punctuation is inconsistent and your vocabulary and sentence structures are both limited. Some of these make your meaning unclear.	